OPEN FIRE

WHIRLWIND PRESS
P.O. Box 109
Camden, New Jersey
08101-0109

FIRST EDITION

Manufactured in North America
Book design by AMY WALSH
Cover art by CYNTHIA BACK
Editing GRECHEN THROOP
and JENNIFER FUSCO
Design assistance KATY JEAN MAY
Jacket photo by ROBIN HITESHEW
Produced by FOREVA PRODUCTIONS
Set in 11 point GARAMOND
Printed and bound by MCNAUGHTON AND GUNN

Acknowledgment is made to the following magazines where certain
of these poems, sometimes in earlier versions, have appeared:

Mad Poets Review, "I Carry The Star"
Mad Poets Review, "Sorry Street"
Painted Bride Quarterly, "We Chose"
Poets & Prophets Anthology, "Hands"
Paul Robeson Festival commission, "Souls Company"
Blue Guitar Magazine, "Nobody Knows"
Painted Word Magazine, "For E.K."
Painted Bride Quarterly and *Long Shot Review*, "Poem for Lizzy"
Critique Magazine, "To Live in Love"

Library of Congress Cataloging-in-Publication Data

Perry, Aaren Yeatts, 1962-
        OPEN FIRE / Aaren Yeatts Perry

ISBN: 0-922827-19-2

This book is dedicated to Don and Jane, to my ancestors who believed in peace, and to future generations working for a world of nonviolence, sustainability, and equanimity.

And henceforth, the only honorable course will be to stake everything on a formidable gamble: that words are more powerful than munitions.
-Albert Camus

Grateful acknowledgement is made to the spirit of all of those whose contributions of support, courage, creativity, joy, love, hope, wisdom, community and action made the idea of this project a reality.

FOREWORD By Lamont B. Steptoe

Aaren Yeatts Perry, *enfant terrible* of American letters, is a poet's poet. He has
so many literary gifts that any writer of the craft cannot help but come away
from his poems empowered and inspired. Perry's voice is oracular, performative,
playful, honest, and infused with a cosmic wisdom and shamanic humor. Perry is
astonishing for his linguistic musicality and rhythms, as well as for his compassion
and solidarity with those oppressed and vanquished by his ancestors. However, his
work is not only historical in scope but also contemporary. Perry's work engages
the time of his time. But even as he duels with the darker forces of history, he
makes time to love and be loved. His literary palette contains the pastels of his
childhood, the deeper reds of political bloodletting, the cool blues of late-night
jazz clubs, and the joyous sunbursts of nonviolent hope and action. Perry's is an
energetic but focused verse. His eagle eye misses nothing. There are landscapes,
crowded stadiums, villages, jungles, and highways coursing through this full-length
collection - our first glimpse into his larger body of writings. These poems
are luminous and redemptive, full of courage and brilliance:

> "...Name's America, I'm a white kid from the Midwest
> born at crossroads in the middle of nowhere...
> I'm Indian massacre moans drumming the road stones
> underneath families out on Sunday drives...
> I know the road. Soon as I could walk I ran away...."
> -Souls Company

> "This is not America. In America no one
> disappears overnight, a pen can't cross out
> a civil right. Dissent is not a terrorist's fight...."
> -The Bones of Geronimo

Perry's lyric resonates Walt Whitman, Jack Kerouac, Langston Hughes, Etheridge
Knight in the broad sweep of its concerns, its artistic vision, and its ability to
give voice to the common man and woman in the struggle to survive against the
corporate paradigm of modern life:

> "...Yeah, I raised a family sweating over that
> bastard. Makes you wonder, don't it, why they shut

> the damn thing down? Yes sir, I'm bitter. Do the owners
> know me? Never spent more than two nights in this town.

> Sure don't send post cards from South America.
> They just looked at figures on a printout; now we've got

a ghost town with a four-lane racing through. All we hear is the
calm, quiet trickle of families leaving."
          -The Stack

From the Midwest of his origins, Perry takes us into the wider landscape of not
only America but the globe itself. Open Fire is not post-adolescent searching but
rather the work of a mature man on his way to the height of his expressive powers:

      "…these are the poets uttering with ripened, sharpened
      tongues what the ghosts of their childhoods told them
      they would one day hear and die saying…."
          -Not For Sale

Perry is global in his inspiration and vision, and personal in his transformation of
these ideals into form. He has traveled since his youth beginning with childhood
visits through Western tribal areas, to his rebellious running away from home in
Europe, to his mature decisions to bear witness in the planet's political hot spots,
such as Sri Lanka, El Salvador, Guatemala, Cuba. His poems vibrate and pulsate
with curiosity, conviction and prophetic intensity. There is genius in the associative
powers of his images, his wry humor, and the overarching truths of his analyses.

      "…Follow the sound of someone
      chopping wood in the distance,
      reach the boggy spring and a boy
      in a steamy sunbeam with a machete,
      sweaty, gasping, says to go back
      to the village. Go home. There is nothing
      here for you, all we make and grow
      your country takes for free."
          -Climbing the Stream

The late writer and folk lorist, Zora Neale Hurston once said, "You got to go there
to know there." It becomes clearly apparent in the poems of Aaren Yeatts Perry
that he has made that journey to "there." He identifies with the victims of history.
He is also an informed witness, sociologist, political scientist, anthropologist
and humanist historian. Not by academic degree, but rather by the passion and
centeredness that he brings to his material. These poems are fashioned on the
anvil of love, also known as the heart and tempered in the open fires of truth.
Perry "frets and smiles" in this "genie bottle full of voices." You will too when
you open it. Read these poems ALOUD for their full effect. Be dazzled by their
mystery and history. Take this book with you into the future. It is my privilege to
announce Aaren Yeatts Perry to America and the world. Heap him with honors!

O P E N   F I R E   *Table of Contents*

FIRE I

I'M TELLIN'

Oh! For a muse of fire,
that would ascend
the brightest heaven
of invention.

~William Shakespeare

I CARRY THE STAR

I sneak across your yard on a thumbnail moon,
slam fate against your aluminum storm door
with a bang that cracks open your dreams.
You never see me but I fold your dead
in shrouds of pressed wood pulp,
wrap them neatly in classified ads.

I am a paper
boy, a paper tiger: black boots, ink stripes,
yellow fur hood in a Green Bay Packers coat,
prowling your turf at night's darkest hour
when only jazz that can't stop and dew exist,
when the smells of wet things reach orgasm
in a distant train moan, and cats square off
in hissing black arches ready to lose an eye
knowing the diurnal do not need sight to see,
when it's so quiet even insomniacs
on porch rockers finally nod off.

No one knows this time but messengers.
Only coons and birds and stars and I.
We go through your trash cans with wild dogs
and mark your zinnia beds our turf. I am the one
who reaches in your window to turn the channel
on the TV you left on all night. I eat the pie
you left in the window to cool while starlings
brief me on your dreams. We all travel together:
animals in the night, paper spirits in the day.

I am a paper
boy. It's not me who comes to collect the bill
for news delivery. It's not me who comes for Christmas
tips while you're having sex and yells,
collect for the Star? Collect for the Star!
Collect for the Star s of Mercury and Hermes!
Collect for the Stars of Exu and Legba!
Collect for the Star of Anubis.
Messenger of the spirit world calling.
Time to pay your dues.

RIB JOINTS ON THE MOON

This was a zone: bony kids shivering home
from watching the most recent row burn down
on a January crack battlefield where playgrounds
swung so long without heat the sun bent its knees
to the pavers not even melting the gray snow
icing these cracked streets lined with leafless trees
and air so thin birds walked south.

This was the moon where, after church,
if we were good, we'd go to BBQ Heaven for ribs.
Outside the window at another kind of church,
wings, butts, booze thawed the frozen tongues
of a dozen old men in parking lot preachment
chattering around Christmas trees blazing
in a 50-gallon drum along with ornaments
heated up enough to explode reflections
like the devil popping his gum bubbles
right on his flaming lips.

Inside, homemade hot sauce burnt our lips,
pig blood moved through our veins. Stovepipe
smoke signals woke the dead sky and I secretly
left a trail of chewed neck bones home, tossed
from the car window so I'd know where to go,
what to eat if called to what I thought was heaven.

I remember thinking we were already there, chewing
buttery cornbread at a window seat, watching steam
saints drift from the mouths of men outside, when
the shiny grill of a '62 Chevy bit through the lot
and sunk its teeth into shattering plate glass.
The only thing faster, the hand of my father lifting me.
How the saving actually works,
light as a salt shaker to safety.

SUNBURN

Summers we used to drive north on white-lined highways
past white-framed farm houses where white-toothed faces
looked out at hundreds of white cows, sucking
the bloated udders of cumulonimbus clouds
until they turned into gray tornadoes.

We drove north to the White M.C.A. camp where we'd eat white
mashed potatoes, white bread, and white meat, and drink white milk.
After napping on white-sheeted bunks, we'd run the long white pier
in our little white skivvies to swim the lake, its surface
shimmering like diamonds just above darker depths.

From the white sand beach we'd get in white speedboats, skip
across breaking whitecaps then sit in the canal's ivory reeds
and catch silver trout, white enough to sparkle. The sun bleached
everything except for my skin, which turned bright red.
I peeled for days: thick gauze, nurse's cabin Solarcain, stinky

balms and lotions. Sheets of flesh were removed and examined
by others who only got darker. Flakes fell like efflorescent brick
off an old building, like red paint curling off a car in desert sun.
I thought it would burn right through to my white skeleton.
I thought I would wake up and find all my freckles merged

into one cooked layer of skin. Instead I woke early from the pain,
found the secret stains of the world's Caucasian affliction the nurse
couldn't cure. A pink mist back-stroked the dark green water
spitting up rainbow trout, a mother of pearl dragonfly eaten midair
by an owl with an abalone oil slick of feathers, a lime chameleon

that would disappear come sunlight, purple and gold sky fading
over smoking embers aglow in night's other camp across the lake.
A white preacher was already up in the white-bleachered chapel
saying, "Stay in the white light." But I ran to my cabin, grabbed
some grape taffy and wrote to my mother in red ink on yellow

stationery, telling her I'd seen myself in a VW window and surely
I was pink. I asked her why adults acted so peachy keen
about it all and how old I'd have to be, how many layers of skin
would have to peel off, before we all turn many, many colors,
shed old skins like other animals, make friends with the sun.

COTTONMOUTH

Because he was quick and deadly on the line of scrimmage,we named him after a poisonous snake.   He could bite holes of daylight through the defense for my up-field runs.   He acted more like Jimi Hendrix.   Corey could play guitar and we jammed in the mythical security of youth and private school.   His short hair spoke a slick language I knew from my side of the river.   And for Nolan, who flanked Williams on the line at tackle, his tones were home. His loving folks were ones we'dgrown up with and loved.   But for six hundred other privileged suburbanites Corey's creamy skin was just the other side of Nigger.

Cottonmouth went elite with upper-classmates who were not without dominion and ruthless adolescent ridicule, for whom Tarzan was enough, and whose lives would pass on pleasant lawns never knowing Emperor Jones. Cottonmouth had come from the city streets where people live close, play close, work close. To them, Cottonmouth looked and acted African. Thus, they called him names, loosely and with disdain.

> The last time I see Corey is in a dream. Jack and I come
> to see him in the classroom where we first met. His face
> appears behind the face of a huge grandfather clock. He
> is gasping in the invisible cloud of carbon monoxide
> fumes he's wrapped around himself. Inside the clock his
> mother's European car is running. He is dying over and
> over again. Black Houdini in an escape trick gone terribly
> wrong, he is dying. He says he's thirsty and has cottonmouth
> from all the poison.

Our childhood was gone. His body tackled forever in a car to which others held the keys. Our own mouths dried up at the thought of his demise. We suffocated beneath the weight of our own freckled skin, howled down the long school halls, sprinting to escape the invisible chimneys of this… smoking behind every school in America… to no avail.

WHITE NIGGER

Sure, I'll pull this trigger
You're nothing but a white nigger
Friend of the devil by any other name
Look at your sons' lips: the same...
       Day a light-skinned Egyptian
       Family and an interracial couple
       Moved in down the block
You're to blame for them blaming us
On them being savages and hard
Your boys are forbidden from this yard
And from playing with my kids...
       Will be kids and even her own
       Were color blind for a time until
       She bleached their bound eyes blond
Until you stop bringing those little
Monkeys over with their shit-filled
Underwear and their sticky fingers
And greasy hair. I don't care...
       Is what echoed down the street
       And crashed into the end
       Of the millennium
If their principal and teacher are black nor
What you nigger lovers and your kind do
Just keep it back, don't let it touch my
Precious little angels, pure and blind...
       The Wade boys sat with delicate chins
       Perched on their unscarred knuckles
       Staring over the fence at us playing
B-ball, listening to Bob Marley's call, full
Blast until the day a Mayflower Vanlines
Truck moved them at last, not one object less
To a place with an as yet unknown address

FIRE, MACBETH AND OTHER THINGS YOU CAN'T SAY

Three things you should never put in a poem: Kurt Cobain,
the heart at the Chicago Science & Industry Museum,
and your grandmother.

~David Wojahn

I thought of you as I watched it
cloud over during the Beastie Boys.
It began to rain on the mosh pit.
Divers bubbling to the surface
of a human mud puddle smashed
their limbs against the darkening sky
over RFK Stadium like slippery
crash test dummies until flipped
to security or sunken in the quick
sand of rockers freeing Tibet
for $70 per ticket and I wondered,

when the index finger of Buddha tapped
a 25-year-old cell phoning Dead Head
on the shoulder with 43,000 volts
of lightning, if she had His number
on speed dial. And, if He spoke to her
right before, how could she hear
His words of wisdom over the din
of rappers slamming Western materialism
with their guitars? Stunned in a sea
of incoming sirens, I thought of calling you
and asking if it was that easy to go
and that beautiful, why hadn't you
just done it, rather than threaten
to jump when I said I was leaving?

It should have been Nirvana on stage
grinding out a dirge for the ritual.
I saw Kurt Cobain with the woman
on a cell phone climbing the brilliant
Himalayan stair, telling her how he was
"bored to death with the music."
What plan was she devising with Cobain

Did she feel like a Lady MacBeth
in the masses or like the spirit
fire between them had grown too large
to ignore and could she come over?
No one else saw the ghost star rocker reach
down and touch her hand. Crowds yelled,
"Fire!" and ran for exits while I stood
in the infield wondering if we secretly
choose our way of dying. Surely it is
handed to us, for who would chose fire?

People hate fire, I said to myself, sinking
in the aural mud of sirens mixing now
with R.E.M., as I recalled being evicted
from the Lollipop Classical Music Concert
in third grade during the 1812 Overture
for yelling "fire" at the orchestra, when
I was simply instructing my friend
and dueling Russian Roulette partner,
Jumpy, to fire his rubber band at me.
Then I was spirited aside during a high
school play rehearsal and told, "one does not
say the name of MacBeth in the theater...."
But today's mob was already fleeing in chaos
from the terror-filled words in their heads,
so I stood in the rain and yelled: "Fire!
MacBeth! Fire! MacBeth! Fire!"

Pumping with their bare hands, surgeons
saved the cell caller, ripped her from the
Tibetan Book of the Dead, and her heart
survived, charred to a roasted marshmallow.
You'd be angry if you knew: I wanted
to go with her to the hospital.
I'd always wanted to touch it,
the actual heart, to walk through it
and get an eyeful of the inside of sacrifice.

But my grandmother had locked me in
a hotel room overlooking Lake Shore
Drive with the TV off — punishment
for yelling: "Goddamnit, I gotta piss.
My dick hurts," from the back seat
of the old Buick she wouldn't stop
'til Chi'town. "You're grounded,"
she shivered, her arm flab draped
over the vinyl, her chubby index
admonishing, "Never use His name
in vain and never speak of your body."

While she toured my brother
through heart chambers tall as Sears,
not a drop of hemoglobin on their hands,
I turned on the TV news and saw a Buddhist
immolating himself on the Capitol steps.
On the street outside, it was August
of 1968 and Chicago horses reared in fires.
One man ripped a star off a cop's chest
and held the flaming six points of justice
toward the crowd of men who looked to me
like my grandmother's photos of Jesus.

I tried to tell Grandma I'd figured out
how some people die for a cause and others
use death to keep from changing.
I was silenced all the way home, her
wagging finger a metronome ticking
through an adolescence of friends'
fruitless suicides. Even now, when skies
open up and adults like you run to death
from love's shocking jolts quick
as kids run for a rock star's autograph
I want to say, "Jump! Go ahead.
Let it out, godamit." But I still cannot curse
the unbelievable violence in His name.

You pray for redemption from this millennial humidity, your jeans
wet cardboard and there, off in the street perspective depths, like a
light in a tunnel, a shock-absorbent capsule of human cargo. Manna
from heaven rolling to the curb in your hometown, somewhere in
history. It's square jawed front: your savior's face, your Max A.C.
ride uptown to work, up to any other heaven but this.

Opens its cathedral doors and you genuflect up, into a medieval
knave, air conditioner broken. Windows locked. Hot as hell. Into
the dark tube of belief, into the fleshy squeeze of contrition, enter the
hairy municipal opening, swim in sweat of the blind, sticky ammonia
of the flock, a slave ship on the coughing sea. Congregational sots
press you into the altar, crush your crotch against the collection plate
token box, your face against the windshield. Virgil in an AIDS poster
next to a "don't spit" sign. Milton taking notes on the driver bent
over the bent world following *ah, bright wings ahead of us.* You should
have walked, levitated to the place you're going now but it's too late:
this bus only takes passengers and the next stop is downdowndown.
5 MPH. 106 degrees. $3 traffic jam. You and I are going all the way.

Move to the back. Move to the back. Move to the back! Shopping
bag calves. Mattisse bouffants. Flaming Tiberino hero strap
hangings. Modiglianni nude necks and pits in your face sweat
unstrung beads that roll into cracks and disappear. Kids are licking
the windows, drunks swaying in the aisles. *And whoever's smoking
that crack in the back better put it out.* Your love letters are falling
out on the Caravaggio of an earphoned skateboard crew of heroin
addict skinheads who finger the maps of needle marks on their arm
veins while staring out the window at the cityscape rapping, *bombit,
bombit, bomb the Whitmans and Franklins with carpet bomb vomit.*

You notice the sidewalk is full of Hassidim and Muslims smart
enough to walk, heads covered, to the second coming, but you
hold a fainting senior from falling because it's the Christian thing.
And someone heading homeless, smelling like a dead animal, just
woke up and missed his stop, but will ride the loop again and again.
We the seated, itching, inch across our town somewhere in history,
trying to save ourselves by making the five and dime by five.
Trying to find a sin to fit in and regretting getting in at all.

HANDS, 1972

Back from Nam, Nick Rand played
quarterback in pickup games.
In the huddle, he pressed his index finger
tipped with a chewed off nail
into his puffy open palm that shook now,
glowed from within, and dirt
from the Bushman's back forty
filled the map of his hand print, burned
his battle plans into my mind.

We were pressed back to an end zone
of poison ivy, dog shit, and rocks.
The Temple boys would run wide, curl inside
to where his wart was cut and bleeding.
I was to run the length of his lifeline
and turn for the Hail Mary at his fingertip.
On three Mississippi, I hiked the pigskin
and ran like hell toward a compost pile.

I turned for the pass, saw his eyebrows
narrow to a dark V on his shaved head.
Striding waste deep in a rice mud paddy,
Charlie attacking him from between the rain,
shouldering a 55mm rocket launcher, he waved
me further into enemy territory. A hand
that blew brains out now printed in mine,
aimed, pumped with the accuracy of combat.
The bullet entered my chest, a soft leather
touchdown at the helicopter airlift
of decomposing autumn leaves.

THE BONES OF GERONIMO (Apache)

In my America, family rode bikes warm evenings
down smile-ridden roads, earnest faces, all breezy,
all creeds, classes, races to the water's edge
for 4th of July fireworks. Watched the sky as dusk
goodness worked us into a Quaker silence filled with
frogs, distant backfires, the impoema of river over rock,
the right and safe prophesy of nightfall over an army
of botanical garden statues: Zeuses, Xangos, Buddhas, Shivas.

Kids, safe in Mom's arms, we dozed sure that the cops
were not brutalizing tenements and neither poor nor rich
were out to get us. But the clarion voices of Indians crept
up river into our sleep and we dreamt wordless letters
from a front:

> *Dear Mom, This is not America. In our America,*
> *no one disappears on overnights, a single pen can't X out*
> *constitutional rights, dissent is not terrorism. We*
> *have been sent away to a wild West cowboy state*
> *for the big showdown at OK Corral. Here imbedded*
> *reporters lap up yellow press pools, mull dribbled*
> *bygones babbled by gung-ho dung slingers for fodder,*
> *grist milling templated slogan singers to topple our heroes.*
> *We stab the priests hiding out with our friends; we scream*
> *at the naked president buffing his nukes, but no one hears us,*
> *or sees him.*

> *And down in a big room, boom after boom scooped out*
> *of war dead graveyards, rattling chains and bushes, witch doctors*
> *sipping from the skull of Geronimo, using his femur to stir, plunge*
> *into throats of the people who claim there is such a place a flag*
> *soaked in petroleum, and light it like any good barbarian would*
> *with flint of desire for messiah, and steel of fear of monsters....*

But we were children then and dreaming. We awakened gasping
at the water's edge, lain out in august grasses, arms crossed over
our hearts like pharaohs pledging allegiance to the sky, fearless
at the oncoming waves of fireflies, bats, night hawks dragging
blankets of darkness under which we took refuge
from the first rocket's red glare.

WHEN IT FELL

My dad had cleared everything out
of the old wooden barn in the days before.
His bald head got tan in the work of it.
He'd taken all the shingles off
and told us not to go in there
because it was no longer safe.
We never asked if that was why mom cried
nights, but he wouldn't look away from splitting
wood and squealing nails.

We just trusted that he knew, like stormy weather,
that something bad was going to happen.
One summer day, with no wind or warning,
the empty wooden barn of their marriage
collapsed, just fell, over. The animals
ran wildly, squawking the way they did
when the pig slaughter truck came.

Over the house, huge heaps of dust clouds
rose straw, feed, and feathers
that drifted into the woods.
Tracing dad's footprints out along the tracks
by the lime bed I found fallout, evidence
left for those willing to blame: letters
saying things I'd never heard them say.
Matchbooks from restaurants he'd gone to
when we were home with mom. Razor-sharp
photos of him kissing a stranger.
Information the size of a fist.

My mother stood at the back window
shucking corn into the sink, and watched
grass grow 'round the tools he'd left
in the yard, and watched them rust.
Sis held her. The boys learned
to sit in silence and swallow
for dessert the cuss words
simmering on the stove.

WE CHOSE

Through an army barricade of placards and hecklers
claiming to know who we were and what to charge us with,
forcing sharp leaflets and slogans into our psychic tissue,
we entered the clinic, filled out forms with ironic questions.
Please describe your relationship with the father.

Sun ghosts poured through bulletproof windows. She laughed,
"fulfilling, secure." The other side was blank, the waiting
room was empty except for a few sleeping men whose eyes
twitched every time they heard the machine grunt
in the operating room of their dreams. I couldn't go in

with her under sheets and lights, alcohol and rubber gloves.
Suction now where long ago she'd have taken special tea.
Instead I sat by the Chicago River, my fists clenching a stone
railing. Tears blurred my face from reflecting on the water.
I couldn't see myself nor the dregs at the bottom, dirty enough

to wash this feeling clean. But I wouldn't have drowned if I'd
jumped, only frozen my ethics about subzero population
explosions of unwanted children, orphaned to orphans.
Teens, poor and thinking, we chose. Now, something cries
across snow-covered cornfields stretching through my heart

land home. And my silence pleads guilty. Our lips
press not cold around a tombstone, but warm at a mile marker
weathering a winter. We get out in her childhood driveway
and go on with our lives. I put a gun to my
memory, tell this to stay out, but it stays.

I TOOK MYSELF OUT

Aloof and coy, always other lovers, never time to talk, I
was shy about asking. But as soon as I got myself alone
in a room, I invited myself out,
       and i accepted!
I'm thinking New York strip steak, I say to myself
       and i say, uh, i feel more like a Cajun catfish.
           We went to all-you-can-eat and I had rib eye, bloody,
heavy on the A-1, mashed potatoes, double chocolate shake.
       but i also ordered a Seitan burger, seaweed, brown rice,
       seven-grain bread, tofu butter, and a fruit smoothy.
I insisted on paying but we split the check. Fair enough.
Then I wanted to go out, get drunk, dance.
       but i wanted to see a movie, take a walk, talk philosophy.
           We had a good chemistry but little in common.
           We met halfway and walked to a bar where we
           chatted, watched music videos on big screen TV.
           People whispered when we talked, stared when we
           danced.
       i'm just trying to get to know you i say,
       talking too much to myself
And I say, yea, well, I'm just trying to watch....
       i kept interrupting.
I told myself to shut up.
       but i didn't
           so we got in a big fight.
       i threw a drink in my face.
That really pissed me off. So I jabbed myself in the stomach
with a left,
       pulled myself to the bar floor with a right,
       stuffed pretzels in my face.
I couldn't tear myself away. I was biting my own ear off.
       and i started pulling my hair out
           when they dragged us out onto the sidewalk.
I chased myself down the street, hid behind a corner,
tripped me when I ran past.
       that really took me out, i say.
And I say, to hell with you. You're gonna get us both killed.
       no, to hell with you!
No....
       Someone stopped to save me from myself.

It's alright, I say. I can take care of this.

       yea, i say, he's with me.

Oh I am, am I, I say. And I turn away

         while i stand there giving myself the finger and mumbling.

         but traffic was so loud i couldn't hear myself think.

I'd really gotten myself mad, so I caught up with myself, put an
arm around me, helped me back to a park bench, reminded me I
meant something to someone. Look, I say, there's a ball over
there. How about a little one-on-one?

        and i say, uh, i don't want to embarrass you.

I did have all the moves and the base line drive.

        but i had the smoking hanging jumper and the three.

            We were about the same height

        but i was kicking my ass so bad

I had to take myself out of the game.

        good game, i say. and i patted myself on the ass.

Don't patronize me.

        why take everything so personally, i say.

        and i called myself a sore looser.

           Hand in hand, steps in sync, we went home to
my apartment.

        i had prepared everything: candles, wine, music.

          We get to the door and

I've locked myself out.

        i forgot the keys, i say.

And I say, well, then climb through the window and let us in.

        fine, i say, but don't be surprised if i leave you out here.

        i was still taking off my coat in the other room
when I saw myself undressing in the bedroom mirror. My hands
went wild. I was all over myself. I came into the bedroom and
asked if I could watch.

        no, i said, just lie down and relax.

            We sipped two glassed of wine, danced in the
            dark together.

        i gave myself a massage,

            then we took a bath, got turned on, let the sex steep
            up and boil over.

I wanted to do it again.

        but i was too tired.

It's all in your head, I say. And I went on about "being one"
with your body.

        but i fell asleep

While I was still talking about us.
            Dreams wrapped us so tightly we woke at
            once.
Inside, I am held by a mother and father in a way
        i never knew i was held and i hold a child
in a way I never knew I could.
I asked and yes, I'd had the same dream
            i'd had. i was beside myself.
            i gotta go now, i say.
And I say, yea, I gotta leave, myself.
            but i couldn't let myself go.
                    And we couldn't sleep.
So I took myself out to an all-night diner
            stared into my eyes
                    in a window seat.

LIGHTING OUT

From Riley's grave atop Crown Hill
        I could see it across White River
grazing by a Mail Pouch
        Chewing Tobacco barn
bare back
        tied up
chomping at the bit
        ready for a rider

        Mornings locomotive steam
from its nostrils drifted towards Chicago,
St. Louis, or New Orleans
        Days you could tell time
by how sun
combed it with shadows
        Night washed down
its muscles
with dew

In darkness, its owners lashed it and laughed
        until silenced by crickets
From its mane of Indiana brush
        Tom and Huck's lanterns
signaled me out to the Territories
        I could hear it snort and bray
and stomp the plain
        waiting for me

LEAVING HOME

I closed my eyes
and jumped
at the slow curve
to avoid the caboose
watchman, the sting
of his salt gun.

Over the hellish
metallic wailing of the train
grinding out of the 20th century,
its extraterrestrial search light
raking the dark scrap yards
of progress, I could hear

my mother's big brass dinner bell
banging against the sky,
see her leaning out
from the screen door
in her summer sun dress.
I could still smell bacon frying,

potatoes steaming on my plate.
But I was seated at the table
of an overturned cable spool
in an open box car headed out
east wrapped in a blanket
of coal smoke with some corn
liquor and a hobo packing
Kools and a Smith & Wesson.

Even the wheat fields heaved
red-winged black birds at us
leaving as if to peck out our eyes
so that we would not have to see
what lay along the tracks
just over the evershifting horizon.

FIRE II

THE ONLY WORLD

Avarice, envy, pride,
Three fatal sparks,
Have set the hearts of all
On Fire.

~Dante Alighieri

A CHOICE OF DUST

You choose a crop of dust living in the city.
All you can raise is dust collecting dust collecting dust.
Some say raisin' dust is better'n raisin' cane
or raisin bread, but you can't eat it.
You can only pick it, in big dark boogers
rolled between fingers into meaty bullets
you fire at the Dust God. But his horses kick up dust
and he bangs the Good Book and belts out a laugh
to spite you in this collapsing tenement
you pay out the ass to cough yourself to sleep in.

Your choice of dust turns your dreams to dust.
Sun magnified by dust at dusk husks your lusts,
sands thrust into moonbeam mists and musks whisking
best beloveds away in fast winds and trysts, changing
masks and busts and even guts to dusts. And whose
fists but your own ghost's grind your pasts to dust?
Through your hair does it not silver star dust comb?
You've chosen the Babylon rubble of Gomorrah and Rome!
Subways explode mortars in the walls of your home.

You wake up and try to look toward the future
but you can't see it for the dust. You try to clean house
but your vacuum spews dust. You hire maids
but they don't do dust. You shake your rugs out the window
but it blows back inside. You buy a giant fan
and try to suck it out, wax furniture, wax even your clothes.
But still it appears. Spiderwebs balloon like clockwork.
And when the guests arrive a mouse runs across the floor,
really only a ball of dust in a draft.

Your therapist tells you not to worry, that you are
billions of dust molecules with water added,
that time and distance are made of dust,
that the universe as we know it is only a speck of dust
on the lapel of a black velour sweater
on a grandmother asleep in a rocker in Des Moines.
She'll find it when she wakes up and, no doubt,
try to flick it off, hurling the solar system
into a dust hole and killing us all.
And you'll have to live with it.

You've made a choice of dust
over clinically immaculate high-rises,
dust over clean ocean breezes and sand,
dust over rain-mud bayou, dust
over mountain gust, thin air. The silent
film thief of breath, a source of death,
a force of change, a test of faith,
a lack of luster, a past returned to fester
and cloud your once clear head
waiting for you to join
so calmly beneath your bed.

SOULS COMPANY Petromadness #7

Name's America. I'm a white kid from the Midwest, born
at a crossroads in the middle of nowhere. This beat-up heart
land of abandoned farms and houses no one comes home to.
That's right: America, like the continent.

When I was younger, my daddy lost his mind and killed some
people. They say he was smart. But money and liquor
drove him mad. Since then I been a loner. Try to forget
the past. I thumb for rides. Twilight and dawn mostly.
I keep movin'. Care less, I got nowhere to go. Neither do they.
Driving to work on their way to the grave. They all ride alone.

Maybe that's why I wander the roads. Keep the poor souls
company. Sometimes I get lost out here. Nothing but time
rushing by. Hot metal and diesel breathing hot rubber on corn.
Sometimes I just am the highway. What's in between
the thoughtless, uninhabited miles is written all over me.

I'm a concrete Sanskrit, a graffiti four-lane looptilooping
neighborhood row houses to shambles like the rotting teeth
of a dog that died biting a hole in the pant leg of the sky.
I'm a turnpike grave yard. A long flat tombstone covering
slave bones. I'm Indian massacre moans drumming the road stones
underneath families out on Sunday drives. I'm a midnight trucker
screamin' Little Richard out the window at beefy tit suckers, poppin'
pink hearts to stay up late on the buckin' bronco of a Mac truck pullin'
forty tons of yellow cake over cloverleaf tombstones roaring
over slaves' trombones, cursing fenced-in land nobody owns

America…America Hum'n'shine. Pleasure's mine. 'Bout time.
Waited so long, my feet turned blue. Sang every song I knew.
Don't mind if I do. Nothin' to lose. Quit once. Couldn't hack it.
Home? No. Far as you can go. Hum'n'shine like

Pittsburgh steel: top down, slick hair, gold watch, gold trim
from South African miners dead underground. Hum'n'shine like
Cadillac whitewalls from a rubber tree rain forest now hamburger
cattle field the exit after the Amazon. Hum'n'shine like
Montana metal: hand-tooled cheap by Detroit daddy of eight
kids hungry after laid-off parents kill each other for a job
with the city evicting their own poor neighbors. Hum'n'shine
like a dual exhaust on a Mustang burning. Teens forgetting.
Beach bound on a Texas causeway, past oil wells shelled
when stakes moved to Kuwait. I, the heave of stakes,
cylinder knife the heartland, rip smoke-swallowing
up the breadbasket, fishtail into great plains mirages.

I know the road. Soon as I could walk, I ran away.
Put as many miles of freeway between me and my ancestors
as I could. Pacific wasn't far enough so I headed south.
Ran every country to the tip of the Americas: lava, swamp
and mesa. I tattoo paved the whole isthmus, perpetuity
of white ellipses. Demonic symbols: "no shoulder," "just a head."

Now I'm sure of it. End and toll we are stranded. Nobody goes
slow enough to think about stopping anyway. And those crazy
drivers? Last guy pulled over said they'd closed up all the exits
across the country and everyone was just driving, looking for a way
out. America. This sure ain't the Autobahn. Sure ain't no Tarzan
safari with a land rover and a girl in a leopard skin. It's the edge
of the only world and planets are scarce. I'm a white kid, lost
and scared to death. My GM out of gas at a crossroads.
Twilight. Storm settin' in. Big storm settin' in.

BLACK AND WHITE, CIRCA…

Men in black suits stand at attention, hold themselves into the mouths
of white urinals at 30th Street Station, shivering their way to work and
war, circa millennium's end. I piss, one eye on the Norman Rockwell

shaving, one on a Keystone cop slapping cheeks with toilet water,
elbow punching a broken blow dryer; checking his watch that has
stopped dead as change hitting the organ grinder's tip jar. Nothing

changes. Black shoe shiners still kneel with the same white rags as sent
away vets and saw some back in '43, '53, '63 – play the dozens chatting
for tips to carry them over tracks to a job at the club making more,

buffing wingtips so shiny bankers can see up their secretaries' dresses.
In the stall behind me, an Amish boy peeped a Black man murdering a
guy in the movie Witness. The natural ability of the boy to choke his

gasps at possible evil now eludes a USMC PFC's sobs. His boots and
duffel bunker him into the Witness stall, where he tries to shit torture,
to evacuate what he's seen. I peep him holding himself in the shadows

of the stall the way his mom might, the way the bronze statue of Lazarus
in the concourse atrium, wings big as buildings, holds a weary traveler
in the floodlights and lifts him limp over families tearing into white rags

before leaving loved ones, just how I was put on a train to war. I know
these cries in the stall from my own battlefields. Only that bronze
angel knows what soiled laundry will unfold when it returns the soldier.

In the men's room, we know what to do with this boy less than a baby,
wailing in the fits by which we all come to know from strangers in
strange places our own type of abandon, our odds of Lazarus helping.

Men and incontinent at holding moments, the shiners and I shrug, heads cocked, eyebrows raised, palms upturned as if holding the organs of fate, one in our hands and one under our chins. Over

the sobbing and the *all aboard!*, a shiner tells me, "we do what we can. Can't do nothin' now. History has us by the balls." In the mirror, indeed we've posed into a yellowing tintype.

"I hope he's weeping," the shiner goes on, "on the dirty boots
of his return, and not at the horrid reveille
of his dispatch."

BREAD CRUMBS

A Nam vet's mouth sweats
at girls fattening pigeons
with *bon pain* croissants.

Still POW, his blue lips
purse, twist around a butt,
needs a light, coughs
fuck you
when I bend down
with a flaming Zippo.

Hungry for rations,
he recoils. Does he think I'm
Viet Cong? Some hellish yellow
Charlie sent to guard his
tortured wrong?

Fetal on a steam vent,
just outside the Federal Mint,
dog tags dangling in a dank dark,
the unknown soldier's empty
mouth sweats at a troop
of schoolgirls fattening
pigeons with expensive bread.

PEOPLE STANDING AT WTC WINDOWS
Notes or Future Anthropologists #3

One of us scraping scars off a sky
One whispers bye on a cell
One prays oh well, and why
Hopes the future can tell
How a skyscraper felt, felled
All windows full of humans
Taping stars far and wide, swatting
Flies off screens, peeling smiles,
Dials and hollers denied, one leans
To fly from our just squeegied perch
In a rose-colored Hollywood Squares
Cereal box one boy dared another
To dump across five billion breakfast
Tables and lost: see a tic tac tower Parish
A Hopper in an hour to a Bosch
Kandinsky ten thousand silk ties
Deep, muting the noosed cries
Of the over-employed inside
The oversized in our final
Moments before being
Printed on double-
Paned thermal glasses,
In a Roman II higher than Mayan
Pyramids whose stele depict
Hearts pried alive, thrown
To plazas below, a dower
Sacrificed for someone's own
Power. Oh, the same eerie way
Window-washer iron-ons
Adorn the stele of Hiroshima,
Nagasaki, except that all we did
Just before being emulsified,
Neck tie-dyed, smoke dried,
Palm piloted sky high, tried,
Sentenced was trucked in pieces
To Fresh Kills Landfill.

BOOK OF MATCHES
Notes for Future Anthropologists #7

It was smoky in Bar Kabul, the band
Too loud, but their eyes met
And she held out one hand

Then both, upside down, fingers fanned
Like some Persian guessing game. He let
His Camel smoke clear, tapped her tanned

Left: a book of matches showing an Afghan
Café with palms. I don't know you yet,
As she penned her number in a shifting sand,

But life is short and I can't stand
Seeing this house of cards as a threat.
I'll go up in smoke if this goes unmanned.

That September morning as the cameras panned
The rubble, they found him: one fist held a phone set
To his ear, the other held the matchbook as planned,

Dialing her from a now faraway land,
Phone lines cut from some impossible debt,
Smoke signals of new love trying to expand
From the palm of his outstretched hand.

LAIN DOWN SUCH SWORDS
Notes for Future Anthropologists #8

And now the poets have lain
      down such swords
as once were their pens
      and once rang such chords
as played wild upon
      the strings of their lyre
before this war's dawn
      called them to retire

For now, the bards will stand in shadow
      recording the awful looks
of those unused to pain,
      to turning for solace to books
We sketch all possible nuance
      in the age-old terrified stare
of these eyes who've just lost love
      to a fury of planes from midair

For now, let mourner weep
      and comrade cope
the way innocents worldwide
      somehow found hope
like kids in Pompei, Capetown, Mai Lai
      turned eyes to fire-filled skies
Salvador, Palestine, Chile, now home
      we shake our fisted whys

Soon we will take your wordless tears
        to the shop for another repair
Soon you'll forget again, while
        we resume our expert despair
Drop your burden at our well
        our break is almost through
Soon we will report in kind
        what you hoped would be untrue

Here is the open flame of the muse
        This is the open forge
Dump your scrap wear in the smelter
        your diamonds in the gorge
Watch as we fashion gold from dust
        a sword from this billow's hot air
Watch as we hammer out crystals from rust
        Heal will on this anvil bare
        Heal your will on this page so bare

NOT FOR SALE

It's a busted, bloody lip time in American poetry.
Bards remove their lenses, put up dukes, double
step a shadowbox shuffle at the word on its way.
The crowd cheers when the champ goes down,
slow mo' ink sweat beads splash from the head,
the grotesque Aquarian groan. Readers wince at
bright bruise, the violet shift from reds to blues,
squint disbelief at a title that can't be held or sold.

The best of our time are in the back of the line.
Lose their teeth naming the new age. Put behind
bars for wearing it on their sleeves like slaves.
Crying for cabs when they used to walk
the bridge the night the odes the words imparted
felt so heavy and golden and cool. Our ears can take
no more lead money for a gesture, cannot bear to bare
the uninsured radiation child into this worn world
of boiling warriors again. The sob of the artíste?

The drunken balladeer? The woe of demented skalds?
No, this is not a drama: liquormidnightslitskirtdoorstep
escapedfirebackalleygetawaysavethedayhappyeverafter
tear or play. Not another love affair, let down your hair,
drive off the bridge into midair in fear you might gain or lose
the gifts looted from the muse, chiaroscuro dope of fame?
No, these are the poets uttering with ripened, sharpened
tongues what the ghosts of their childhoods told them
they would one day hear and die saying. The miracle
lyricists piercing tyrannies with fearless Creollo clarities.
Rhapsodic revolutionaries drowning with voice and ink
any dictator who would silence free verse.

These are the troubadours, singing down the walls of silence
and dancing in the rubble. Saxophoning down the walls
of silence and dancing in the rubble. Singing words free
and dancing in the rubble. Singing words free, words free,
words free words, free words, free words, free words.

BY WAY OF INTRODUCTION

"I'd like to preface this poem by suggesting a little
disclaimer that, while on its face it may appear cohesive in form
and content, it is actually two poems sewn together at the chest —
call it a congenital twin — two heads and one heart, making sense
to itself, yet ultimately at odds with the world. And, not
to confuse you, but…"

By this time the poet's introductory comments
had reached so far from her poem that the audience
had not only begun to shift, re-cross stiffening legs,
shuffle flyers about upcoming events in laps like
candy wrappers crinkled during a funeral eulogy, but

"…just to let you in on a little secret, in section three, the obscure
foreign names are those of the ancient Greek and Indian two-headed
deities of selflessness and narcissism. Allow this to deepen the duality
metaphor, a reference to East-West spiritual tension hoping to mirror
and allow us to peer into our own internal, say, split."

the crowd had also become periodically fixated
on the pierced and tattooed Medusa-haired sisters
at the espresso machine in the cafe in the next
room, leaning into the steamed-milk pitcher, pulling
the wand in, out, giggling.

"Earth and sky, and you will notice them throughout, are used only as
linguistic slingshots to project two of Heiddeger's four elements of
reality out across the text. And just one more mile marker to watch
out for as we work our way through this poem:…"

The fans appeared to be looking at the reader but
instead were inconspicuously craning their necks
to see something else: from where I stood, hiding
in Travel and Tattoo, I could see, out the picture
window just behind the poet's head, a television
glowing in the living room of an apartment
on the third floor of the building across the street
from the bookstore.

"…The Corsican baths with the terra cotta tiles were, just so you're
not in the dark, Mediterranean precursors of the modern bath houses,
the first swingers if you will, unisex salons where nudes in steamy
repose revealed from beneath Egyptian cotton towels their fleshy
Hellenic physiques as if each were the other's model *and* faithful
voyeur."

By this point the latté girls foamed so loudly in the café that the poet
could no longer be heard. But this mattered no longer since a man in
boxers and a woman in her bra and panties had appeared in the
picture window (unbeknownst to the poet), their sluggish, pillowy
bellies flabbing about as they roughly embraced one another, back lit
by the strobing blur of a huge Panasonic, both wielding beer bottles
as if intent upon knocking the other to the ground.

> "As much from vanity as from a need to be
> understood, these early exhibitionists bathed before
> and after matches in the coliseums, ample
> opportunity to be viewed intimately *and*
> by their public."

The only thing more appealing than a poem unzipping itself, stanzas
to the floor, disrobed to perfectly lined flesh — the two sweaty tenants
silhouetted before a 48-inch screen, jumping up and down, slapping
high-fives and chest slams. From between their exalted parts,
distorted by electric blue, emerged then disappeared the massive,
arms, legs, and long hair of two Championship wrestlers flinging their
bodies off the elastic ring wires, one leaping into the other's face with
both jiggling butt cheeks, in slow motion.

> "Is this why, I'm sure you're asking yourselves, the
> early Christians invented an omniscient, spying
> God, not to keep evil deeds from being committed
> but as a truly attentive witness to those deeds?"

In the bookstore café, a latté girl hammered open the cash register
with a *ching* as the TV ref in the strangers' living room pounded
the mat then rang the bell and the woman in her underwear finally fell
upon her mate. The poetry crowd applauded the takedown,
shocking the reader awake from her interminable preface:

> "Thank you. Thank you. I hope that these N.B.'s,
> or *notas benes* in the Latin, will eliminate any confusion
> on the part of my audience. And, so, by way of
> introduction, I would just like to leave you with the
> following epigram to begin...."

WHEN WORD GETS OUT

Monday news boxes
　　toppled by a 3A.M.
　　　　windstorm of drunk
　　　　　　teens with no voice
　　　　　　　　hang open,
　　　　　broken. Their jaws
　　are Dali paintings, melting
　over curbs,
leaking a ticker tape
　of American poetry
　　　supplements reviewing
　　　　　themselves page by page
　　　　　　　into the shredder
　　　　of a fire escaped sky.
　　　There: DuPlessis pirouetting in
　autumnal thermals. Berg up to his
neck in the murky Schuylkill.
　　Sanchez pushing down police
　　　　barricades around City Hall.
　　　　　　Perelman blanketing a shivering
　　　　　　　　body asleep on a vent. Olsen
　　　　　　　face-up in Logan
　　　　　Fountain. Weaver sneaking
　　　over the blue cobblestones
　　of Elfreth's Alley past Wilner,
　　emerging under a haiku of fallen ginkos.
Djanikian, a Sufi ghost lifting over an L platform
　　and twisting down the tunnel. A single mother
　　　　wraps a midnighted diaper in page 22,
　　　　　　smashes it into Poe's iron gates.
　　　　　　　　The local *enfant terible du jour*
　　　　　　folded on herself, trashed and
　　　　shivering like a printing press
　　at the feet of the Ben Franklin Bridge.
A flock of up and coming, inked wings spread,
fly through the Whitman's spanning fingers.

Tomorrow a Vietnamese vender in the Italian Market
will wrap fresh monk fish in a W.D. Ehrhart
      and an old man will unwrap it in his kitchen,
            see his hometown alive again,
                  while, in a cursive plume
                       of irreverent anonymity,
              a table of contents listing
         like police blotter a menagerie
             of unknown brilliant locals
                will be cremated
                           in a smoky drum fire
                        at a closed up factory
                  next to the Delaware River
          by a circle of bored teens,
      illiterate and rubbing hands
   to warm up before going
to tip news boxes
      in a windstorm
         into the street.

NIGHTSHIFTFACE

Tug's face was made of crumpled road maps
depicting deep gullies, train tracks, short cuts
his family took from West Philly row houses
and beat two generations smooth, walking
to the refinery for the night shift.

Midnights my way home from Yellow Cab, we'd pass
on the dark sidewalk of Grays Ferry Bridge.
He'd stop and tell how the valve had burst.
I could hear the incinerating explosion. His face
glowed in the same methane stack torch-light
that had branded him with molten crude.
While we smoked, our eyes met through the sulfur smog
blurring his carved mask enough for me to ignore it.
Then I'd run home across streets so slick with petroleum
they could go up at any moment, dual exhaust pipes
and tires screeching his industrialized name.

Tossing at night, I can see the disassembly lines
beneath the eyes, his brows and nose bridge burned in
over a street-cornered frown, the hairpin skid marks
around buckling potholes, jack-hammered lips under
reconstruction ramping down to the curb of his jaw.
The tangled gulfs of his Arcoscars aflame
in a Halloween of flashing red signs.

Danger. Capital. Flammable. Men at work
with their faceless teens, conscripted to war
in a single ignition. The gridlocked
timecard of human endurance. Tears
down the dotted line. Punched out,
with nowhere to go
but back to work.

THE STACK

See it, big smokestack atop the slag?
Biggest of its kind in the world.
Used to call it The Hill. 585 feet tall.

Higher'n any building Phillipsburg'll ever see.
Butte clay through and through. Walls
four yards thick. 600 million bricks.

You could drive a sleigh of horses 'round the top.
Hell, you could drive this Greyhound bus through the flue!
Whole generations of miners quit union jobs

to build that old smelter. Sticks out like a sore thumb
in the sunset, don't it? Straight as a nickel press line
at the Denver mint. Yeah, Montana men digging Montana

metal. Smoke and fire and hot air. It's all theirs.
You bet your ass, flesh and blood.
Ten people have died in those pipes.

They say they come out in the copper. My uncle
was one of the first to go. Dumped a bucket
of boiling hell fire right on top of him, like a ladle

dipped into the soup of the sun itself. Couldn't find him
so they cleaned it up and melted it down again.
Now you just hold a penny up to the sky and think about that.

Thing's a monster. Who knows how many tons of cord per year
it could spit out. Yeah, I raised a family sweating over that
bastard. Makes you wonder, don't it, why they shut

the damn thing down? Yes sir, I'm bitter. Do the owners
know me? Never spent more than two nights in this town.
Sure don't send post cards from South America.

They just looked at figures on a printout; now all we've got
is a ghost town with a four-lane racing through.
And all we hear is the calm quiet trickle of families leaving.

I MIGHT JUST HAVE TONIGHT

I might have
        A sweaty head and be grinding my teeth,
        Clenched fists, and show up jonesin'
        For chemicals when you're not ready
To kill
        For this
        Habit I have
        But don't
Somebody
        Let me out of detox
        My brother never came to get me
        So I walked the bridge
Tonight
        To get the blue line down to
        Bazooka Street for some ice
        By myself and oh, yeah
I just might
        Be shaking and bending up your mailbox
        Or fence while I'm asking for change
        Through bloodshot eyes or breaking
        A few windows, you know how I
Have to
        Get that train
        Or I crack
        What I don't want
To kill
        'Cause I need some change, something
        Warm and fresh, some blood,
        Some flesh — I need to know
Somebody
        Is gonna
        Come with me
Tonight
        To the other side

FASHION MODELS POSE in Street Person's Grave

By day, White girls pose
in this factory alley alcove
sporting hundred doll rags
knifing their jeans
to seduce the rapist
in every consumer
into this cute soiled grave site—
       anorexia Americana
       on location
       resurrecting history's vampires
       to marry these chicks across
       the bricked-over threshold
       of their death wish.

By night this was a Black man's bunker,
Where until last Tuesday, homeless
Gerald kept warm burning trash
inside this hidden stoop, cooking a dog
       on a foil grill over a milk crate,
       its plastic trickling down
       his stone bedside.

Back in the day
such pococurante Caucasians
whipped such bony Black men
to load out bulk chocolate
from this factory dock
       now fireproofed
       photogenic urinal
       for such scatological
       parasites who

this morning would have shot him
just as he is: last night's forty, cardboard
blankets, his toothlessness a gap ad in itself
for the new spring urban guerrilla line
had he not frozen to death, hosed out
            early today by city workers
            like stagehands prepping
            a movie set.

Tonight soul transparencies of street-lit media
whores will autosuperimpose in dark glows
next to Gerald's ragged ghost and he will cook
them a pigeon shishkabob over a low
newspaper flame. A chilling double exposed
            negative will emerge in some darkroom
            developer: a man and four women starved
            by prosperity, swallowing the lean
            into a vortex of tan lines, soup
            lines, race lines.

ARMIES OF CLEANING WOMEN

Everyday
in a quiet
furnished mansion
in a quiet
gardened suburb
a quiet woman comes
to mop the floors
and hang the wash
and polish silver
and collapse
in heart attack sweat

Everyday, mothers
of mothers in battalions
of domestic troops
armed with blue fluids
scarfed in paisley
march from buses
to battle the dust
of the rich
and feed their dogs
only to fall, heroic
American casualties

Sun-draped corpses
spilled beneath
leaded crystal panes
Another mess to clean up
before trudging home
to crowded
noisy tenements
on crowded
noisy streets

WAR CORRESPONDENT

I am writing from the heart of occupied territory. Gotta keep it brief. Things are heating up again. We lost thousands last year. This is the country with the ninth highest murder rate in the world. I hear gunfire now, also voices of women interrogated by their torturers. They don't speak of it, so that they can live to feed the kids.

Unfortunately, I've grown accustomed to the automatic rounds ringing at night so that I can now sleep, sometimes. Accustomed but not immune.

I keep writing reports by masking out images of tragedies I have seen — bodies of slain leaders marched through the streets, victims of the drug war wander aimlessly in and out of buildings, prostitutes emaciated from disease, miles of bombed out... well, you know, the usual third-world landscape. The drug lords and weapons dealers have a hold on the money. The terrorists are on TV everyday, striking fear into the hearts of hard-working people, and the neofundamentalists run the "public" schools.

The signs of a people under siege are everywhere. This country hasn't established a democratic process that includes the entire population. I don't know how long I will be here on this assignment. You know, your training tells you to tell it like it is. But your editor tells you that the public just isn't ready to hear the way it is.

The truth is hard to stomach. Coming up on one of the new legalized police road blocks. I have to put this away and file some stories. Tomorrow's another day. Gotta go. More later.

Much love, Ciego   ~Philadelphia, PA USA 2004

HOLY VANISHING POINT

A nun's panties and anklets drop from a clothesline
to the dunes and whisk away in the winter wind.
Her blue habit aerials down the beach, gets tackled
by a fisherman's hat skipping on shore like a swallow
from the whitecaps. Still pinned to the line, her bra
and slip wrestle with someone in the silicate gusts.
Were these left by the Sister I saw from the lighthouse

skinny-dipping her blocky body into summer's last tide,
a couple watching her from the stones of the jetty?
Was she possessed, ridden seaward by a tide of ghost-women
Drake brought to this mansion after oil made him rich enough
to build a train line here from Philly? When the Sisters
of the Sea went south did she lock up and lift off, stripped
ascending the lattice of swirling sand?

Now the squalls are climbing sea walls, chewing like sharks
on the long wooden rails, once far from this beach.
On the red tin roof, a weather vane rooster points northeast
like a crier in the fog, lit by a flashing yellow beam,
summoning the lost from Atlantis. Even the fishermen, Peter
and Anthony, walk inland, defeated sentries ignoring the Cape
diamonds washing up at their feet. It is dusk at the end

of an era, the entire State a shifting dune.
Slippers and stockings run down the foaming shore
searching for Sisters to fill them. Fifty
empty rockers rock on the second story porch
of the empty summer home. Like wind on the lips
of beached whiskey bottles, their wicker backs hum
the salt-healed hymns of the celibate.

SORRY STREET

One block up from Sad on Angry
Sorry Street cuts into Nightlife Boulevard
at the same angle she'd look at me
when she wasn't telling.
These days I pass by without a glance.
I can't see down Sorry anymore.
Been blocked for months.
Power's out, sidewalk's piled with
the impassable rubble of costly repair.
The blue cobblestones of Pity Alley
buckling down there under blinking
sawhorses. That's the corner

where we used to play this game: her
in the street light standing like Stella
staring at me starring on stage, smoking.
She'd tell me to come back to her,
push me away when I did, slap me
for trying, cry when I said I was leaving,
see if she could stand it when I stayed.
Then we'd kiss and say, sorry.

We used to do shots 'til Paddy's Pub closed
then hop scotch stoop to stoop down Sorry,
all the way to Drunk and Rage.
We both wanted out but couldn't see it.
Now I wonder if it's her smoking in one
of those tiny tv-lit row house windows,
her face blue as an alien; or if
she finally met someone special
down the Agony Steel plant.

I just came back for one last look.
Tomorrow I'm moving out
of the Inner Doubt section
of town all together. I can't even see
down Sorry anymore.

FIRE III

BOOK OF MATCHES

Ojala que no fallamos bajo el peso y el calor del fuego del mera corazon que nos maneja.

I hope we don't stumble under the weight and heat of the fire from the very heart that drives us.

~Nineth Montenegro de Garcia

HOW TWISTED SMOKE

How twisted a barber pole
How twisted a candy cane
How twisted smoke rises
      Like laughter above a fire
      In the face of a heavy rain

How twisted the tracks
      Of the windiest mountain road
      Disappearing without a trace
How far the fall
      And of the torturer making his victim crawl
How twisted the smile on the face

Feel how your throat twists
      And swells when it tries to muffle its cries
This is how twisted god is when
      Wrapping the blindfold of war
      So tightly around our eyes

DISCLAIMER

The pictures in this book
Are by combat photographers
And were shot right before they were
Shot. The images contained in this book

Exhibit certain graphic footage not suitable for children,
Women, grown men, or anyone having recently eaten,
And for those who cannot stomach the stomaching
Of the stomachs of the poor by the hungry rich.
Yes, that is human flesh.

And this teenager lying here is the only one who survived.
The army soldiers who took the kids to the firing
Squad thought he was dead because half
Of his friend's head landed on his face.
He now lives a short drive from here.

The full-color action glossies of this older
Woman adjoining these poems help you visualize
Elements of war that words simply cannot convey. For
Example, this cropped and screened telephoto composition
Imagines with its blurred face, perhaps your relative's head
Covered with this leather bag, her skin
Covered with those cigarette burns, her toe nails…

By now you have looked away, even closed the book
So as not to see her fall from the chair unable
To utter something you already know: that
It is useless trying to understand the pain
Of war, even if you paid for the movie
You think of it as with your tax dollars.

The closest you'll come to sympathy,
The best thing you can do for me now,
She tells you, in this caption, and rising
Up from the floor with no eyes and blood
Dripping onto the floor, is to honor
This suffering by seeing every moment
Of your privilege, during which others live
The unspeakable, as a time to work towards peace.

MOON SKIN

Jungle crows
have plucked out
the moon's eyes.
In equatorial black night,
scalped him alive.
They have dragged
his huge skin,

      a silk sarong woven
      of peacock feathers,
      tears and human
      teeth and bones
      inlaid with burning
      car tires full of kids,

over a nest of pearls
in the Bay of Bengal
to hide it from
even the gods.

      In utter darkness,
      they patrol its borders
      seamless with sea
      screeching its secret
      name: Sri Lanka
            Sri Lanka...

TO EAT DIRT

I kneel eastward to kiss the living earth
that bore me
but am made to bend and eat dirt
now steaming with human blood.

I wanted to build
mosque next to church
next to synagogue
with the sacred stones we now throw
at the madmen staring through
history's cross hairs
as they riddle our children
with rubber bullets.

We could have been brothers
and sisters, on both sides of this river
green with adrenaline, our eyelids
hanging together at night like ripe figs
over the same cup of tea, our skin
aging anew, alike as Muslim, as Jew
in these arid valleys.

I wanted to kiss the living earth
but was made to eat dirt from plates
of red hot barbed wire.

Now the borders between us
crack open like neck bones
in the teeth of desperate
hunters for land.
One reaches the boundary
of what one cannot say
and many throw into
history's canon barrel
the caustic, flammable
stone they used to build
condominiums on our tongues.

CLIMBING THE STREAM

A woman weaving a Mayan blanket
dangles her feet in the stream.
A fish jumps in a pool and she
pulls tight the loom.
The sound of a man sanding
a handmade wooden dresser
mixes with water whispering
what it's seen, and you step

up the rapids by a vast hillside
bean field where men bent over like
hairpins cling to folded rows of earth.
Further upstream, a mother and child
fill a bamboo doorway underneath
an old Coca Cola sign. Inside
someone spreads avocado on a *tostada*
and you slip on a rock. You stand
to look and she smiles, offering you
the child for one thousand *quetzales.*

The stream narrows, steeper
under double-canopy jungle.
Spider-web-covered waterfalls
lead you to the mountaintop
clearing: mossy ground cover
with fallen wild oranges, limes,
avocados and violets.

Follow the sound of someone
chopping wood in the distance,
reach the boggy spring and a boy
in a steamy sunbeam with a machete,
sweaty, gasping, says to go back
to the village. Go home. There is nothing
here for you, all we make and grow
your country takes for free.

THE FAIR: REVELATIONS OF SAN SIMON

It's better to run and get shot in the back than be captured
and try to endure it. There is no unuseful pain.
~Nineth Montenegro de Garcia

Burnt hair and corn smoke haze
roof a mud corral.
Cattle fence their calves
in barbed wire nerves
A horseshoe blinds a dog.
Farmers dervish from coals
burning fire iron snakes
into Palomino hides.
Black bulls flee screaming up the valley
and raise hair on the neck of *Volcan de Fuego.*
Here in Chimaltenango, even animals know
it is better to run.

Workers return the fair's aching steer to graze.
From corral up to the village,
six men climb cobblestone streets
past pinball and taffy stretchers
under a Ferris wheel churning
against a wind of refried beans.
Owners shoulder a wall shooting rum *Inditas.*
For the night feast, three pigs turn
and get shot in the back.

Up the hill on the corner, Indians genuflect
on the steps of the church of San Simon.
Inside sufferers' candles burn: blue wax
a wish for work, yellow for health, black....
Tobacco smoke climbs a sunbeam.
Believers cure their pain in rum, then
look to the camouflaged mannequin saint:
a man in combat boots and army fatigues,
booze and flowers at his feet,
dollar bills and *quetzales* in his hands,
open-palmed under the black vinyl holy symbols
of Miami, Liberty, Disney, New York.
The walls adorned with plaques in thanks
for favors received. Better to join and forget,
to appease this relentless deity of violence
than be captured.

Tonight accordions will grind
to hands clapping tortillas
and sequined *mariachis*
will turn their *guitarrones* to the moon
at wide angles to hide mothers
emptying still emptier coffins of the never found.
Some will turn stones in the dead of night.
Some will dance 'til they drop and try to endure it.
As if there were no unuseful pain.

WHEN IT RAINS

Here in these mountains
named after the son of God
no one can save you
from the dust and water.
The weather's always changing
and umbrellas are useless.

Here, when the lemon orange sun
and sacred word sky turn
to black metal and open wide,
the rain falling from storm clouds
isn't moistening bodies, filling
glasses to fill gullets. It's made
of lead in blue, white, and red.
When it rains here,
it rains bullets, bullets.

And the mud sticking to the legs
of children running,
running, isn't soil for sewing corn,
carrying rivers. It is brown skin
and blood mixing in puddles of
bad weather where parents
swim without life jackets, sinking
without the very savior.

WITNESS

And the sun rises over an ash volcano,
strobes through bus windows, grazing
the heads of sleeping passengers en route
to Ilopango airport. The only one standing

for the ride, I know no one
really sleeps in a landscape posted for war.
I straddle the aisle, grasping the luggage racks:
arms as if crucified, head to one shoulder.

I drift off to the farewell of a woman hovering
over the mountain outside. Her blue hood faceless,
arms akimbo, hands holding a heart-sized diamond
at her solar plexus emanating sharp starlight

that jolts my head to the other shoulder.
She leans forward, whispers to me, *"hable, testigo!*
Speak, witness!"* and thousands like her appear
in a sunrise agape dreamscape: blue robes, arms

locked symmetrically into a honeycomb chain mail
of brilliant diamonds turned mouths now breathing names
in a wind the pitch of jet engines. I cut my hands
from the rack and the disappeared disappear.

ONLY GOD

I come from revolutionary Nicaragua
with these songs for the people
of Sor Maria del Transito church
of San Pedro La Leguna, Lago Atitlan,
Solola, Guatemala.
I cross the water with the word.

It is said you bring arms in your words
over the darkened borders at night
to Guatemalan guerrilla in the hills.
Are there arms in your words?

Only God. These are the words of a people's God.
Guatemalans bare their own arms and hands and face
the future with a history made of corn and jade flutes.
These are songs of faith for the hands and ears
of the people in the church of Sor Maria del Transito,
San Pedro La Leguna, Lago Atitlan,
Solola, Guatemala.
I cross the water with the faith.

It is said you bring revolution
to the workers in the fields
over the darkened borders at night.
Is there revolution in your faith?

Only God. These are the songs of a people's God.
The *campesinos* travel for months to turn the land
and want to make their own revolutions and work.
These are praise songs and hymns for the wishes
of the workers in the fields on the hillsides
above the church of Sor Maria del Transito,
San Pedro La Leguna, Lago Atitlan,
Solola, Guatemala.
I cross the water in praise.

It is said you bring communism
to the Indians of Guatemala
over the darkened borders at night.
Is there socialism in your music?

Only God.
This is the music of the people's hope.
The indigenous survive their struggles
with their own social ways and beliefs.
This is music for the struggling believers
in the church of Sor Maria del Transito.
I cross the water believing in God
for it is only the people's faith
that can solve the problems of this land.

DAYS OF THE DEAD

In memory of the Dead they cook sweetbreads
and dip them in coffee and black beans.
They make candy out of the Dead and eat it.
They concoct pink *fiambres* from
cow, pig, goat, fish, chicken, frog,
in red beet sauce that rings the lips
of those that bring the Dead back to life.

Kids make the Dead into kites and fly them
over the town like national flags from hillsides they loop
in and out of the vultured sun. Children stand
on food stalls and tin shack roofs in the open market
place and fly the Dead on strings with colored streamers
in the dusty wind that rings the town
that brings the Dead back to life.

They animate the Dead with flowers and smell them.
Mountains of bundles and woven wreathes of the Dead
are sold. Rising from pine needle street carpets
orchid pedal rainbows cling to thick air, pollinate
ancient cobblestones where mourners in dark veils
and suits, kneel with large crosses and prayers
turning the Dead into songs and singing them.

They explode the Dead from a canon at Calvary Church.
All-night fireworks sound the coming of the Dead.
People come from miles to see Christ's coffin
float on the shoulders of a hundred men in black.
The march of the Dead blares from military tubas.
Horses, lantern bearers, purple-robed followers
lead the coffin through the streets that ring
the town that brings the Dead back to life.

Every day in the name of another saint,
they try to swallow it, fly it up, stamp it out
in the streets, sing at it. Every day they chase it
to the edge of town in long black processions.
And every day when they get home, its tired face
is waiting to bed down with them for the night.

THE CONQUEROR

Duke's last flick
Was an explosive,
Wild, wild Western
With Susan Hayward
And a glowing cast

The Conqueror shot
In the Utah desert
A year after Dirty Harry
Staked it out in mushroom hat
Clearing out six thousand
Unwanted sheep and some Indians

Location scouts never saw
The invisible celluloid
Of true grit, the real American
Graffiti left filmy on canyon walls
Duke's six guns and monosyllabic

Machismo were no match
For Harry's magic A-bomb dust
B-movie goers didn't have a clue
Until two hundred extras went chemo
That the Mushroom Hats were immune
From justice and that the Gip had moved
Hollywood to Washington

Leaving whole states
Of Leukemic Indians
In barren reservation hospitals
With no movie theaters, scalped

VIET NAM VETERANS MEMORIAL HIGHWAY

Maybe Dupont felt guilty.
Perhaps Westmoreland had a bad dream.
It could have been Nixon's nose
wouldn't stop growing, so he ordered a sign
to relieve himself on the wayside.

A small sign on Highway 95 outside Wilmington, Delaware
on a bridge that arcs over a vast defoliant oil slick
in a spent-gas-drum moonscape lagoon of agents orange,
white, and blue. Spilt milk. The stuff that dissolved the V.C.
and the balls of American youth.

A tiny plaque honoring a generation of trained assassins
sneaked home like package bombs for families to disarm.
A reminder not to look down into the shiny
apocalyptic war mirror where 70,000 deaths
shimmer in liquid graffiti names ready to ignite.

A sign flashes by on your way to the beach.
What did that say? "Vietnam Veterans Memorial Highway"
The fine print inferring: "No Americans were in Southeast Asia.
It was all filmed right here in the polluted waste lands
of Delaware Bay."

Just a sign. The receipt for a corporate write-off
to comfort mothers on their way to mass funerals in D.C.
where more traditional war memorials
are being unveiled
just in time for the next U.S. invasion.

BURNING BUSH

*It's amazing I won. I was running against peace
and prosperity.* ~ G.W. Bush

Chkchkchkchkchkchkchkchk. Child-proof Zippos flicker in crack
houses across America, sparking tiny bushfires that glow the boney
faces of the future. You hear the eerie echo of flint stealing, the
Arctic wind of it sucking the feeling out of pure pink lungs:
whwhwhw, Kgkhkgkhkgkh, hahhhhhhhh (inhaling, choking,
exhaling): blowing the lights out of the mega sega play station
movie set kids think they're in...

In mom's kitchen, already pharmaceutically zombied babies' blood
shot eyes bug out just before popping into their fruit loops.
Slobber and snot trickles down the chins of swirling death vile
sippers into their lunch boxes, the zipper of their mouth in a bunch
waxes around the exhaust pipe of a bic pen or car antenna and they
inhale: whwh, hahhhhh... ready for school with a pb&j, a beeper, a
semiautomatic and a lighter for starting bushfires: chkchkchk.

bushfires...burn in vacant lots across a map of disconnected dots,
wh, ah, the demand in the deregulated market place of laid-off
fathers who beat up their mothers whose sodomized brothers sell
their desperate sisters who spend the change from tricks on nerve
candy imported by bushes and designed for kid pushers who burn
kids in bushfires. See their brains burning like twigs, like methane
smoke stacks over Texas oil rigs? bushfires, chk, wh, kgkh, hah....

You could get a killer high burning and rushing the bushes' ranches
in Colombia or in the golden triangle in Laos or in Afghanistan.
You could do something, like vote, if you could turn off the tv:
chk, or get off the cell phone: chk, or log off line clicking here: chk.
You could lay your body down in front of the dea or cdc or
fda or cia or nbc or cbs or abc or cnn or pbs if you could find it,
your body, your conscience. Chk, wh, kgkh, ahhh...but

no, you're in a drive-by, shooting glances down ghetto alleys, chances are lost not found and not too far down from where you eat and bed. Your eyes connect without respect to the reds of the dispossessed eyes of neglected stick figures inhaling the shadows and you shake your head, but the image stays inside instead like a glowing crack hit chk, wh, kgkh, hah.

Why torture yourself? Why warm your hands on brothers torching brothers burning sisters burning mothers? Why burn any other when you could burn some bush? bushes burn so nicely wrapped like a Carolina stogy in a U.S. flag. Need a light? Mississippi's still burning. Here's an ember. Remember? Philadelphia's still smoldering. And look what they're shouldering in 'Bama: Birmingham's still aflame? If you saw a burning bush, not consuming itself quickly enough, you could help.

Strom burns so nice. Jesse could melt some ice. A bush or Lott's wife baked in a beat up flag or smoked on the BBQ broiler of the Liberty Bell is so much better than a thousand needle points of darkness igniting the epidermis of a nation one family at a time: chk, wh, kgkh, hahhhhhh.

LOVERS ON SAND

He shook in mid-ecstasy, his balls popping like Hersey kisses
Melting on the Bermuda triangle of her Bikini atoll
As Hiroshimas went off above and below
Her quick atomic tan line.

She thought it was Him her Slow Thighs rose
To meet, seven feet above low tide
On an island deserted with second comings.
It was really only the Pentagon at a "Crossroads"
Evaporating two hidden lovers browning
In a honey moon on a beachhead
Dior would later name swimwear after:
Bikini! The new look in '46!
Elimi / native! "Dress to beat the heat!"

Forty years later, Franky Goes to Hollywood
"Dressed to beat the bomb." He and a lover
Lie on the beach waiting for Calvin Klein
To name the military necktie he wears,
"Nagasaki-old-hat-who-cares?"
And to call his innocent socks,
"Alamogordo-me-mores".
Girls waiting to see him still wax-rip
Their pubic hair off in a 20th-century
Mating game so they can wear up their crack
The G-string of islands where nuclear fallout
First caused balding: a turn on.

When the U.S. explodes in a bi-kinetic firing squad
Of meteorite souls fleeing into the antiworld
And California's jaw hits ocean bottom swallowing
Beach lovers in an electromagnetic pulse wave gulp
It won't be a test. All the Gucci, Izod, Christians'll be gone.
But Franky'll get a thing named after him.
The nuclear winter will clear in 2525
And some Rough Beast, thinking he's in Bethlehem
Will find Franky's radioactive underwear
Washed ashore in what was Reno, sniff it,
And name the new L.A. ocean front, "100% Polyester."

THE DAY AFTER

Psssssttttwwwwwaaaaabbbbbooooommmmm!!!!
PostWaaaaarBoooooooooooooooooommmm!!!!
Post War Boom? Won't be a Post War Boom the day after.
The day after it'll be night. It'll be night forever the day after.
A long night, a dark night, a cold night, a winter night,
A nuclear winter cold war with no winners.
No heat, no life, no love, no welcome back soldier.
Ice age cave men battling with clubs for hip bones
And soup cans and tampons and soda crackers
And dehydrated water. The living will envy the dead.

Push the button! Push the button! Light the fuse!
This won't hurt a bit. What happens in the final hour
Will take but a minute and there won't be a second
Chance.

The day after, the President, out of martinis and air
In executive bomb shelters will emerge from the rubble,
Movies in his eyes: "We've won! The world is ours!
A kingdom...of ashes.... Laura, was the Little League
Diamond damaged, what are the TV ratings?"

And then he'll feel it, the boom of a war economy recovering.
His voice will thuddddd against radioactive silence
And he will collapse under
A boom of darkened rain,
A boom of ice and bugs,
A boom of frozen children
A boom of voiceless shortwaves hissing, "come in, come in..."

And in a gloomy hollow nothing boom of doom
His hair will fall out, at high noon...boom.
He'll reach for his six guns but there'll be no one to shoot for it.
"Cut! Cut! Cut!" He'll yell, an understatement in the dark.

The day after will be night. Forever-space-black-eternity night.
The humble returns on our investment in death.
And other planets will be banning bombs and banning war
And taking notes and filming as we whiz past them
At 186,000 miles per second:
Psssssssssssssssssstttwwwaaahhhbbboooommm....

WHILE YOU'RE SLEEPING

though earth's now drawn and quartered
phone lines sprawled through jungle trees,
even in the hills of desolate countries
that would make the hardest soldier freeze

join with Kahn and cross the Kyber Pass
you'll have joined the living dead
you'll wake to find your body, yes
but that they took your head

they'll take your loved ones too
away in horse drawn carts
you'll cup your tears in bloody hands
and cough up years and hearts

in hands that once wrote songs
in hands that once plucked strings
then your prayer fists will fight
and ring the mourner's song
and sing what the mourner sings

for what you'll see when you wake
will make your bones reset
make you as Kipling warned want to
roll over on your bayonet

THE LIBERTY BELL

Psychedelic balloons bob against Independence
Hall and tourists coat their fingers
with pretzelmustardcottoncandyicecreampopglue
then move towards the bell in droves to stroke
the crack: the obscene anus of North American pride
millions flock to ooo, ahh, and photograph.

You can't ring the Liberty Bell but you can follow the crack
down the Mall to Wall Street, to Three Mile Island seeping,
to Nebraska missile silos, to Silicon Valley teetering
on the fault line.

From there, it runs South, deeper and wider, a trench
the CIA live in, eating Salvadoran, Guatemalan, Nicaraguan
families for breakfast.

The same crevasse cuts a maze of copper mines
Dictator Pinochet hides Chilean workers in.
It is the crack of the whip by the driver of the slave ship
Philippines, lacerating skin paths for revolt.

It slices underground rears its cracked skull in Sri Lanka
then quakes through the surface in the Middle East,
spurting U.S. crude oil and others' blood into the desert,
slams into the Kyber pass and turns away from WWIII,
rips down the African continent with an abyss so deep,
Apartheid cavemen still keep whole nations enslaved in it.

The crack is a scar, a gash, a cut, a compound fracture
in the skeleton of life around the world. It is a bottomless pit
in which heritage henchmen deal crack to anesthetize
social change, a black hole that sucks cultural life
into the antiworld of consumerism, greed's deep hatchet marks
around the trunk of the planet and back

to D.C. cracked jokes and leaks, cracked-up heads of state,
the President cracks his lips and Armageddon jingle bells
dribble out on our children from the broken home canning jar:
justice spoiling on the shelf. Back to our God of War statue
tolling silent death knells from the lobby of U.S.A., Inc.

The bell's an old dead pear left on the square to split, rot, and dull.
To smear and fog the fingerprints of emigrants who picked it,
and not wax clarion glory, and not sing praise hymns.
It cannot shine or swing: a perfect monument to the mute chimes
of Freedom. A bell with a crack the shape of a tear.
The impotent voice of a nation, crying without even cracking a note.

The Liberty Bell can't ring anymore but if you listen hard
you can hear people singing *'Tis of Thee*
and falling through the crack
pledging allegiance.

PASSPORT

From her knees she stopped me
in front of the very cross
of the National Cathedral.

Will you marry me?

I don't even know you.

But I don't want your hand,
your heart, your money, no.
I want to be an American,
free of this terror.

I am already married, I tell her.
I am wedded to the struggle
to end the terror. I am wedded
to that fire in those mountains up there,
to that corn. I am wedded to the dead.

Oh, you're a priest?

No, it's that this passport is a shovel
to unearth the disappeared.
It is a map of secret grave sites.
It is a handkerchief for widows' tears.
Note the stamps from around the world.
I will marry you if you take this
time bomb of skin color, the guns
of my eye color, the map
of my passport to Washington,
and bear witness to help end the terror
from which you pray for holy matrimony
to rescue you.

SMALL WORLD

The world is too small here to fall
in love so I become enamored
in steps. It's an age-old problem:
when I fall in love but she, so pure,
cannot and doesn't catch me falling,
I hit the ground hard. The pavement
splits under the weight of the heart.
The impact causes earthquakes
and everyone feels it. The family
worries if her injury is Catholic
and rumors fly through the air
like black crows over garbage.

No one falls
in love here. So I walk
carefully to the fountain, sit
gracefully on the bench and watch
the sun that somehow sets without falling.
A ray of auroras fornicates with distance
without dropping her curtain horizon.
The park lights up, revealing
lovers embracing like statues
leaning into darkness without
toppling. Even the night crashes
down on their shoulders without breaking.

I can't fall in love here. So I
put my message of love in a bottle
and throw it out to sea.
But the world is so small
that the message returns
through the faucet
and into my cup of coffee.
I fall to the table, swallow hard
and study in Spanish
how to become enamored.

FIRE IV

PEACE FIRE

Unless the eye catch fire,
The god will not be seen.
Unless the tongue catch fire,
The god will not be named.
Unless the heart catch fire,
The god will not be loved.
Unless the mind catch fire,
The god will not be known.

~William Blake

BACK TO THE FIRES

And so the people came back to the fires
      Left the buildings empty
As the buildings were empty and cold
      Abandoned their sprawling homes
As their homes were abandoned and old
      Put down the poisonous food
As the food had made them sick
      Tore down the walls and fences
As dividers had silenced their voices
      And came singing open fire!
Back to the open fire

And the parents who had said
      Go up to your rooms
And the siblings who had said
      I hate your friends
And the friends who had ignored
      The wishes of their loves
And sent them out in the cold
      Called out to the lost, open fire!
Come back to the open fire

And for a while the skies were filled with smoke
      From the fires that burned through the night
And for days the flames leapt higher as folk
      Tossed away what had caused them fright
But soon the air was clear again
      And full of the smells of the earth
Those who had sung at the open fire
      Had found their inner worth
Sang without fear in their voice: open fire!
      Back to the open fire

ARIKU: A RE-MEMBERING

Listen.... Listen to them playing.
Listen, It's Legba. Listen, it's Exu.

Ariku Legba. *Ariku* Exu. Ariku...
Bring them back. Return through the flames.
Dance home now through these words.
Ariku a los mártires de las Américas, Ariku....

Listen to the voices embodied in the spirits of Paul Robeson,
Rosa Parks, Fannie Lou Hamer, Harriet Tubman, Martin and
Malcolm. Bring us the bodies of Nat Turner, John Brown,
Denmark Veasey, Ché Guevarra, Luis Real, Tecun Úman, Seattle,
Black Hawk, White Antelope, Sitting Bull. Crazy Horse,
Tecumseh. Call upon Jack Rabbit. Coyote. Crow. Crowd this
room with smoke and drumming for the nameless millions.
Name them. Know them. Feel them breathing.
Let their breathwind stoke this peacefire. Feel its heat.
Call them now: Ariku a los mártires de las Américas. Ariku.

Bring us the gouged eyes of the Cherokee, so we see trail home.
Bring us the severed ears of the Maya, that we may hear quetzal.
Bring us the severed hands of the Aztec that we may plant.
Bring us the severed genitals of Africa that we may create.
Bring us the severed wisdom of Asia that we may teach us.
Bring us the severed souls of Europe that we may love again.
Bring us the severed tongues of the Tahino that we may sing,
ariku a los mártirtes de las Américas. Ariku....

Let dancesweat moisten thirsty throats of their exile in desert
winds. Let these drum calls fuel their journey down blood streams
of the Americas until they overflow. They are rising. Rise and
flow, now rise: *ariku a los mátires de las Américas. Ariku...*

SPILT MILK

In Memory of Benjamin Linder

Every time you rub your temples, trying to remember
a name or kill a headache, you touch the soft place
near the hair line where the bullet entered Ben, a guy
a lot like your son, brother, father, at point-blank range

and turned off the light he'd brought to rural kitchens,
not so different from the kitchens in your home town,
Ben's town. Cross hairs trained on him each day
while his palms full of sun warmed up farm tools

in towns like yours used to be where machines never barked
progress down dusty roads until someone like Ben came to work
softly in the spring, armed with love and knowledge to build
generators to bring power to people who knew what it meant

to have none because they'd had theirs taken and took it back.
And Ben had helped by juggling, clowning on one wheel,
making Virgilio and Consuela laugh though their daughter
had just been disappeared by the amputators of tongues

and fingers and breasts that like to gather with knives to scar
the newly healed skin of independence. Over the slicing
and shooting you could hear them slurping, siphoning kids
to feed the volcano as ransom for raising barns and towns

soft targets like Ben bring light to: El Cua, San Jose de Bocay,
with main streets shorter than U.S. supply planes.
But their darkness found no place to stay, for Ben had started
generators for street lights and medicine refrigerators and

lit operating rooms and recovery rooms where the wounded
revolutionaries laughed and healed. And though tears
of milk flowed into burnt soil from unsuckled breasts
flooding a continent, Ben had built a dam.

GRACE LIFTS US
For Claribel Alegria

How many battles won with only minor gunshot
      Wounds to the body politic,
To the body. Electric, the armies of
      Human spirit survive
Under her watch. She commands a flourishing
      Flower of rebellion
To pollinate on wind and trail. Silently
      In class, in library,
Troops of her Words, hybrid and distilled,
      Know to march boldly.
Stanzas of hibiscus ground cover, whole
      Coyunturas of Frijoles,
Maiz, arroz grow like edible silk phoenixes
      From the volcanic ash
In the valleys made of hair braids and furrowed
      Brows of those who love the land
They work. How beaten down time must feel
      In its hopeless fox holes
With Generals like her.

Some warriors succumb to the counterrevolution
      Of aging while she still climbs
The defoliated mountainside battlefields
      Of the stage — actual grace lifts to us
Instructions. In a clearing, erect
      At the outcropping of the podium,
Looks over her glasses. In one hand the pistol
      Of a fountain pen, in the other loafs
Of poetry like bread. The shiny machine gun
      Of language strapped to her back,
Bandoleers of honesty crossing her chest.
      The bullets vibrating
To the ready on her word.

HE SPOKE SPARK

For Etheridge Knight

He laughed lightning.
He cried conflagrations.
He no'd napalm.
He coughed coals.
He fussed flames.
He imbibed embers.
He tongued torches.
He cussed candles.
He spoke spark.

If you drank the gasoline
Of racism at every meal
And for sixty years your words
Were made of flint and steel
You too would turn
Fire-breathing dragon for real

And you'd laugh lightning.
You'd cry conflagrations.
You'd know napalm.
You'd cough coals.
You'd fuss flames.
You'd imbibe embers.
You'd tongue torches.
You'd cuss candles.
You'd speak in spark
with words that light the dark.

BIRD
For Charlie Parker

How does he play like that, and why do they call him Bird?
the monks ask as we sit near a four-thousand-year-old
Buddhist temple sipping hot tea, spitting Betel juice
and eating rice with peppers so hot the mind burns open
to its primal core. He learned to breathe into pain,
I tell them, until he lifted off. He's been flying

across history ever since 1952
when this Kansas City horn player,
Charlie Parker, made some music
he recorded in Sweden in 1954
that was remixed in New York in 1960.
After changing the ear of a generation,
that music is being broadcast on shortwave radio
from London, and heard by a Philadelphia poet
born in 1962 in Indianapolis now listening in
from an island outpost in Sri Lanka in 1990,
with some Biku monks, to a sax that will always
remind him of home — at the turn of this century

and the next. Bird will still swing free from a radio cage,
singing equatorial rage with his heat waving wings flapping
heat waving wings up and down sax keys, ineffable
phraseologies possible only with a breath
taken centuries ago, the beak of his bop horn
pecking open the shell around time itself to feed us
with the tender meat of sounds rarely heard

in this world. Keep calling, Bird. Keep
echoing love calls across shortwaves forever
forward into history. Satellite dish
to satellite dish keep nourishing
our empty souls you ugly brass Pterodactyl
morphed into futuristic auralflash.
Keep wailing, keep wailing, wail the anguishing
wine songs of human sorrow out into the ear
of the galaxies until they hear and answer back.

POEM FOR LIZZY

Phoenixes rise from South Bronxian ashes you warm your hands on. This heat brightens your markers, sharpens your pencils, loosens your brushes, shakes up your aerosols for the night shift when you will art revolt. This volcanic brick by brick-a-backwards meltdown of imperialism's fractured reactor is your muse, is your stage. You are the Curelian photographer of the no-longer, recreator of the gone, escort of the dying to reincarnation's door, entropy's hired portrait painter.

Kid Lizzy: graffiti man, you burn commuters' newspaper eyes. You vomit Park Avenue's greasy money breakfast all over Cadillac windows. You stuff the bounced checks of subsidized housing back through Wall Street's pinstriped coffee lips. You speak fluent languages the U.N. won't recognize because your words realize the situation and laugh graphic anuses back at midtown's grotesque face. Out in the drunken bug-eyed gossamer American dream brain, you shit art at them. Everyone wants to see it but can't through constipated, hamburger-infected rush-hour balls. They can feel it though, the heat of it. The sound of your sparkling boozy colored prophesies playing off MilyMonkyDizzyLizzyTrane cars that click passed in seconds, counting off the stolen and numbered days of these streets. Your paint can is a time bomb, a depth charger that rusts a hook in the craw of these notorious animals in their murky selfish dominion. Skips a fisted beat into their clean time with thick lime, black and pink quick strikes coked full of "Lizzy" all over urban walls. You drip fire on this dried-up bankrupt system they call education. Illiterates cheer as your words moan up the flames engulfing corporate billboards while you swing art cages around Babylon's lying necks.

Your fshshshshshshshshsh. They can see it glittering in the nuclear glow. They try to censor your shkshkshkshk but you're gone, eatin' chunks of chocolate night, autographing city rats' purple rule, tracking crimes to open-mouth scream poses you snatch and stroke back to life in wall-rendered mosaics of cum and blood. Cum and blood? They didn't want to see cum and blood but they get it back anyway in a vogue reflecting pool of the wishes of the poor that cries out in glistening sweat-script depictions of "change:"

Credit cards appliquéd with machine gun stitches
to the bankers faces and to the kids of they bitches.
Home boys tap dancin' on their very heads,
blood tricklin' down to the graves of their beds.

We want change, not charity. Change:
Refugiados marching on Capitol steps
with photos of the never found.
American cityscapes burnin' red
against a twilight background.

We want change, not charity. Change, 'cause that's all there is on these streets they left you on with nothing masks, masks, masks could hide. Nothing textstextstexts could explain. It's all over, this city of jazz. The one you rainbow projectile back into the face of the prison guard of capitalism that cages your innocence.

Your cry is heard! From the Battery to Harlem. From Howard Beach to Bensonhurst. From Newark to Watts to East L.A. to West Miami. From the walls in the prisons at la frontera to the walls in the camps of the Altoplano of Guatemala to the walls in the homelands in Soweto and Bofuthatswana to the walls in the West Bank and Gaza, your cry is heard. *Tu llanto esta oido. Tu fuiste visto anoche corriendo salvaje por las calles de Loisaida, buscando amor, buscando calor, cuando no hay coro. Pintando rythmos caribenos en estas paredes sin sol. Pintando sol. Pintando rojo, verde, amarillo, azul matador a sacar el dolor de esta oscuridad. Pintando negro elcaballo blanco de la cocaina. Pintando cerrada las casa de crack with your spray gun syringe. Tu llanto esta oido denunciando dictaduras.* Your cry is heard!

Your brilliant crayon bomb strokes riots across Houston, across A, B, C, the Bridges, 125th and Lennox, swiftly swabbing New York's rich wax eyes with ether. Name after name, scarring death to life in subway stone bowels, across rooftops, down 42nd Street. Scrape sky, scrape sky, space craft screech traffic to a halt as you tear a rip across the split pea sludgey Hudson and lift off through the smog into outer space: "L-I-Z-Z-Y" cut out into Jersey's wired, wired sky. Connecting the stars with an aerosol jet stream of frantic Arabic curls. Manhattan's discolored heart dripping from the shiny teeth of your name.

METAPHYSICAL HOUSECALL

For James A. Baldwin

Your third eye glows in the dark
of my living room, cracks framed glass,
freeing you from the black and white photo
of us standing together in an elevator
ascending some cityscape

Like wine splashing
from a shattered crystal goblet
you arrive again, flying in from the France
of dream, wearing the mask of night
you steal into the battlefront
quiet of my home jingling
Johnny Walker ice cubes
and smiling like a drunk Santa

I would think this visit strange
had you not also appeared to me before we met
in an elevator roof shack playing cards at a table
with Gary Snyder, turning from whiskey
and winning, pulling down your cheek flesh,
rolling your great prophetic pupil to the skies
and writing a Chinese calligraphy letter
on the white of your eye that meant,
if you choose to be a writer
many strange and unexplainable
meetings await you

Your leathery hands palm the spines
of my books and finger the dust
Your gap-toothed grin stretches
the length of the moon filling
the living room wall
And your eyes bag the copper and silver,
absorb the flicker of candle
flames for your journey
to all the hearths and homes
where your books open

BEHEADING DAEDALUS
After Jack Myers

I leave the concert early to ascend
and instead see Daedalus smoking
a Camel on the porch again. Always

that shifting father face, apparition
in an elevator or diner window
offering broom and dustpan

to clean up my redundant downfalls.
If as a teacher, he knew that the perfectly
carved mask of parenting he imparted

would be deformed by the sun, melted
by the pyromania of youth and by gravity
be trashed with equal swiftness earthward,

would he still excise his likeness,
hand me such a taxidermy? He signals
a cigarette, wordless through the breezeway

and exhales a carefree ghost that kisses
his bald cranium, rises up with it, carries
his shiny dome over to mine,

his silvering beard, my own before
I'm ready. His regal profile, one pane away
standing in the shadows. My own body

side lit in a linoleum hallway between
a phone booth and a Coke machine,
reflected in the mirror of the glass

door to the other world. His head
overlaid upon my own winged body, fitting me
with a crown, for flight closer to ground.

BRUTUS AND MANDALA BREAKING STONES

For Dennis Brutus and Nelson Mandela

You were tattooed property
chained in hell's clown stripes
dragging boulders from the brine.
Even the sun abetted Apartheid
in weighting the mallets
they lashed you to wield
against chunks of your own will.

Like deities gifted with
some siren fight song from the surf
your quarry chants fashioned
clubs into Olympic hammers
for pulverizing prison walls.

The din and the drumming
of your gavels and your words
crumbled shackles in a stone age
and your freedom tumbled forth:
shimmering paths over the muddy
swamp of war, laid with the hewn
diamonds, the tender pearls
of revolution.

ODUNDE

22nd and South Streets. 100 degrees in the shade.
Oxun sweeps through me, and the sun turns cool on my skin.
Ice cream and mango peelings dissolve on the street griddle.
The air is a hot onion cut open. African market steaming,
incense pouring, straw hats and dread caps turning.
Shishkabob and ginger punch. Copper and brass
sparkle and love fingers that touch them, tongues tasting festive.

Odunde! Odunde! Drummers cross polyrhythms.
West African sixes mix the steps of street dancers
turning a soul turbine, gathering momentum.
White robes and scarves merge into one unified wave,
push and sway in a pulsing procession to the river.

Yoruban drums via Bahia vibrate the South Street Bridge.
Via Bahia Yoruban drums tremble the Schuylkill River.
Beads, gourds, and drums shake: "casheshe, casheshe,
low, low bass. Agogo, agogo, shakere, clap.
Shakere, agogo, shakere, clap." Bright flowers and fruits
are soaked in gold beams of honey, blessed with ritual chant.

Bata drum tones open spirit's mouth. Oxun
swallows falling rose petals. Delirious fetishists
throw shoes, dollars, watches, candy, food to her.
Stirring bodies in white Condomble gowns see an arc
of hazy light and Exu brings up the answer:

> A large Indian black woman at the railing of the bridge
> takes Oxun into her body. She begins to shiver.
> The men take her slippers. She waves at the river,
> Lifts her skirts and shakes her head, pacing.
> *Ohhh, puey, puey, puey, ahhh. Ohhh, puey, ahhh.*
> Inside her, Xango makes love to Yansa in a lightning storm.
> She splashes talcum powder on her face, paces and faints,
> paces: *Ohhh, puey, puey, puey, ahhh.*

Oxun returns well-fed to the shimmering
river. On her face a smile mosaic
of fruit rinds and flower petals
flowing towards the Bay of All Saints.
It is a new year in the African world.

TO SMELL SOUND

For Sonia Sanchez

Oh, to smell her blues rifts floating up
like rib song smoke from a basement bar
To smell her horny salsa pulse from radios
for lovers embracing in central parked cars
To smell the salt of her conch shell
blast like gun powder over a festival crowd
To smell the raga of her tabla chant
whispering so loud

Is to smell two cellos blossom and bend
then wonder what they said
To smell the warm milk of a balladeer's
trumpet-line as you lay down for bed
To smell the sex of a flute trilling
out windows like fresh baked bread

To smell the bubbling soothsayer's voice
and know exactly what she means: if
you could utter such aural soul you'd feed
the world with violets, oranges, blues, greens

Oh to smell her sax breath read a story
about things lovers can't say but dream
To smell her notes fall like rain, to smell
them scream, to smell them hit hot
Harlem hard, to smell them heal
the heart, here, and steam

WHEN THE JAZZ GOES AWAY

For Amiri Baraka

There's always a line or two of Baraka-tones left in your ears
a dose left dizzy in you dances and shivers
and you can't shake it, like they do.

When Shepp and Roach and Murry and them lift off into space
the quiet aftershock is like a sound proof booth after Saturday
night in Manhattan and you feel like pouring straights
to augment the gap they pried open in your musicality.
When the magicians leave the set their spell wishes
you had T-Bone or J.J. tailgatin' you home,
Bird flyin' upside your head. Maybe Philly Joe Dukin'
and Countin' on you, or Don Pullen you by the ear
across Billy's vibratoscapes where Miles of Trane freight
flatten predictability like old coins. But they leave

and you lie on the tracks. You're ready to give up your house
and car for jazz but you know you can't keep it so you start hearing
Chet Baking blue correlations through a toilet plunger.
Jimmy McGriff/Smith hundredseventyfifth notes
squint sweat barking from Earlen's fat eyes on a church organ.
Cleanhead and Lockjaw howl up Loisaida alleys and chase you
into hobo fires. You love the alto cab horns and break skids
but you need Max's wrecking ball to demolish
all dentist office music around the world. A subway
squealing into the tunnel Getz Dizzy, meets Puente
and bends a radio in half, steps off minor, bumps around a third.
You want Art to Pepper Cherry and catch Sunny as he falls up
scales, all words falling to pieces, and "Sounding" lines
and symbols crashing into the moon light of your alone blues.

And in a moment they're gone. And when they go away
you want all their records and books. You want to make sure
they like this planet as they could choose such things.
You look around on the stage floor for pieces of lung
or lip stuck to reed or fingers turned sax keys
or bass strings stopped in chords or pools of dripped notes.
But they just disappear and what they sweat just drifts downtown.
An octave follows you home and you sound like it.
You dream you're conducting the dialectic of silence
but you wake up and your head's as clear as glass
notes they played.

SCATTIN' IN THE SHADOWS

I am home
Under these street lights when it happens
My ego alters and
Everyone that's come before
Hangs around the hall
Drunk with melody they never fall
Leaning at angles up the alley wall
Then follow me home
When I leave
Limping in a six/eight

At a good intersection
We can break it down
Into blue green yellow a capella bop
Slaves to the music
Playing dozens in a barber shop
A cop stops traffic from laughing for
Our toe-tapping parade
And we do an octave up from
Be do dee do dee do dee do odes
Primal codes

Sounding out lighting
For the cast we are
Staged in vacant lots
Directed by griots'
Choices, we six or seven pass around
A genie bottle full of voices
On a moonlit highway

Where I solo Holiday
And on a milky way hilltop in southern Indiana
Or street-lit truck stop in N'Oleans, Louisiana
Or leaking from a shortwave in rural Montana
Or jumping in a juke joint in old Atlanta
We're Bix, Hoagie, Louis, Chet, and Miles
With a bandstand of trumpet bells
That frets and smiles

NOBODY KNOWS

"So, you ask me the name I'm known by, Cyclops?
Nobody — that's my name."
~Homer, *The Odyssey*

Nobody hears a garbage truck's breaks moan
sees its great jaw open at him, thinks a G.M.
wouldn't eat Nobody while no one red in the face
as a discus thrower heaves up trash bags full
of sleeping vent men and rich-people leftovers
into the crusher Nobody hears the bones snap
in its teeth while no one else at the wheel smokes up
the dawn-bloodied eye of the windshield with a cigar,
puts it in gear and Nobody runs for the train

No one knows but Nobody's been up all night playing
jazz piano and Nobody's delirious, wondering if
anyone is lonely or is everyone busy trying to be someone
they ain't and maybe find somebody who is
No one could stand to be with Nobody
if no one knew what Nobody knows:
that no one's got a lot to look forward to

Nobody owns much so you don't see Nobody trying to fish
pink dolls out of dirty rivers or lining his pockets with
Admiral Wilson striptease tokens or all-night diner silver, no
Nobody got work no one'd want: to speak silenced lyrics
sing earth love songs to halo the saddened lovers
Nobody knows with daybreak moonrings

Nobody wakes his woman whose rose tipped fingers
point out the window at all the cyclopses driven
into the tunnel by some force Nobody can name
and speechless lays down his swords and dreams

Nobody knows any better but nobody doesn't worry
because if somebody out there says I love you to someone
and no one hears it, Nobody knows they'll be all right
Nobody understands because Nobody cares
Nobody's been there and returned
Nobody knows

DON'T TAKE YOUR EYES OFF THE SUN

I went to Cuba with a gay priest to find my woman
who said if we ever became separated to look for her
in my favorite place in the Caribbean, but she ended up
showing me how the past presents the future its orders.
We hailed a '59 Rambler with a Russian diesel and
hand-tooled pistons made of old train parts, and clunked
to the outskirts of China Town where we bought
25 Cohibas and 25 Montecristos for chump change
fresh from the black market. Orlando the cabby fired
one up and said, "Look, my position is life is short.
You want the $8 lobster, you go for it. You could be
an Egyptian slave, a German Jew, a Kosovar Albanian,
an Afghan refugee. You could be born in a country at war
and spend your life running from bullets, but what you do
while you're running is your choice. You want to spend
your life chasing women? Go for it. But go for the $8 lobster,
not a tuna sandwich." The priest looked at me like a crustacean.
"Forget it," I say to the priest. "You ain't no catch."
"And if you think you deserve to suffer," Orlando added,
as he took another long drag on the phallic tobacco stick,
"you will. Taste this fine leaf and forget about the past."

We took a '58 Hillman with a Mother Mary hanging
from the rear view mirror to the National Theater,
watched Alicia Alonso's Ballet do a millennial version
of Carmen with the good old love triangle unmasking itself
in front of the crowd in the grand Garcia Lorca room.
"You see," the gay priest slipped in, "she doesn't ever leave
a man, she just shows off to another one so they can dance.
Men shouldn't be slipping on a man's blood for a woman
or a man. Jealousy is so twentieth century." "Thanks,"
I said. "I like my pain. Look, there she is: 4th row center."
But by the time I had descended from the balcony to the lobby
I was back in a crowd of 1957 beehives, zoot suits, gold crosses
and pearls around the necks of rich couples rich since 1757.
I bowed my head, walked the medieval cobblestone alleys
slaves laid, past troubadour mariachis serenading the Corinthian
columns and balustrades. I stood like a statue of Don Quixote
in a Gothic doorway, its arch pointing to the National Cathedral
steeple pointed at a guy in the sky who looks like Hemingway
and I wielded my fountain pen, stabbing my eyes at her passing

incarnations. "Fencing windmills again?" asked the gay priest.
"Who's your daddy?" I said. "If you'd seen her in morning light
after a love night, you'd think you'd met Jesus and had him too."
We took a '56 Edsel, wing tips and running boards to Old City.
We met his boyfriends for a modern drag show, knocked off
shots of *guarapo* cane juice and Havana Club rum at the Hotel
Hemingway. "Have you ever heard the cannon fired?" one asked.
You haven't seen *fresas* y chocolates until you've met the tearless
eyes of a gay Cuban doctor or lawyer on the Moorish castle's
granite guard towers overlooking the great Havana Bay. Here you
can see like a crystal ball into colonialism, Legos of history
crumbling over dusty maps and fallen walls. "The few standing are
the oldest..." he says, looking at me. "The ones in the mind — the
Western mind closed and opened by Spain each dusk and dawn so
as not to dream. This bay was sealed at night, a cannon fired, any
slaves still at sea, hanged at noon. Each day the bay opened and a
cannon was fired. But the greatest cargo barges on unseen. Notice
the bay is a mouth, the throat deep, wide; the lips small. Cubans
do all you do, think all you think, but say little. In *machista* Spain,
married men keep a lover boy. For U.S. youth it's the sign and seal
of rebellion. You think you hurt looking for your woman? Here,
it's treason if I find my lover. If love's not occult enough, man-
love is simply

counterrevolutionary. We took a '56 Ford, with doors
that wouldn't shut to the Hotel Inglaterra. A hooker in red
dress, red high heels, red lip stick and purse at a checkered table
cloth on the patio said, come up to my *paladar*, I'll show you
a rumba buena you never knew you could know, a *dulce
guaguanco*. It's sink or swim here, and salt water kills my hair
so let me sink and show you my handy work. No, next week's
too late to come back. I'll be working South Beach Miami
by then, sending checks to my folks in Santiago. How many pair
of shoes do you think the woman who left you would demand
before coming back? I only have two: work shoes and work shoes.
You think free health care, free education, housing, and food is all
I want? Variety, boy. Run up a credit card until I die of variety,
then ship my body back here to be buried, these same red shoes.
I'm a Communist; you can write "good old days" on my grave.
But don't tell me what to do for a living. Sin is older than this
bread; they don't call it pan magdalena for nothing. Have a bite.

I said, *Cuidate, chica, ciao!* And we took a bicycle
ricksha to a dusty barrio on a Saturday morning when 100
kids were rolling wheel rims down bumpy stone streets
under the dripping pendant flags of the country of laundry
strung from balcony to rooftop antenna and flapping
in the sunny sky. Shoes resoled where a beeper salesman
might be; greens with tops by the pound at a wooden stall
where a 7-11 might be; a father pedaling a bike to the park
with his wife on the fender and his son on the handlebars
where an SUV with a car seat and a cell phone would have
passed us entering a Rec Center where the Zen teacher said,
"Here. I am here, and nothing more. Be present and find all
you are missing." We did Yoga Tai Chi with Cuban seniors
who showed us their prayer room: six foot Xango with an ax,
a bottle of rum, and a plate of flowers and honey. "This is
Santa Barbara," one said. "If you ask and make an offering
they will help in your battle." I laid her picture on the altar
and as I crossed myself,

I felt a horse-drawn carriage sweeping me back into history,
Cortez laying waste to golden fields to find gold, torching
Aztec aviaries to prove a reach longer than the condor, leveling
thatched roof huts to build shopping malls. I woke from flames
with the setting sun in my eyes on the wall of the *Malecon*,
waves crashing into fanning plumes the size of sailboats.
A boy fishing from the wall stared down his homemade line
into the broiling brine and spoke to me: "if you stare at that sun
as it goes down, watch it disappear, you can talk to the woman
you miss, she'll hear it; don't take your eyes off the sun.
There are ways of talking to those who are far away," he said
as the clouds around it swirled into dancing drummer. I remember
looking behind me at hundreds of men and women staring at the
sun just before I faced it. I stared into the melting orb. It was dark
when a cabby called out from the street. "Ice at Coppelia's?"
I asked and he laughed, "Two lines at Coppelia's these days,
Yankee. One for you and one for Cubans. I don't have all day."
We debated the economy and tourism dollars.
"I'll buy us both a piña ice cream," I said. "We don't have time
for neoliberal reactionary bullshit," he said. "Everyone works...."

We hopped into his '99 Mercedes and headed for Vedado: "Come here and cut cane in the blazing Guantanamo sun, dance, break bread with some farmers. Raise a child on rice and beans. I might be a Commie and love it; I might hate Cuba so much I'm ready to windsurf to the Keys so the Pope can dictate what I can and cannot do but if I found that woman you're looking for, married her, I'd take her to New York, show her the same exact number of people who live here on this island wondering how the hell they're going to defect from that one. And I'd tell her the same thing: everybody's got an answer about love and revolution but no one wants to admit nothing's perfect in either. At least we ain't slaves. Here, nobody has nothing. Think about it. It's what you make with what you got. See those waves crashing against this old stone wall every day? Time can't change this. Just like love, you can't fight it, you can only hope you get on its good side and make the best of it. You'll be lucky to find her at all. Sometimes these animosities between beautiful people go on for forty years at a time. Find your gay friend and thank him for putting up with your crap. That kind of camaraderie is the closest thing some of us ever get. Love must be defiant to beat the tyranny of alienation. We all just keep floating on like old battleships at the ready, fighting for love, fighting to love…thorn in the lion's side. David, yes. David, he says." Don Quixote, maybe? I ask. "No," he says, "don Ché Guevarra. It's defiant love. It's David, it's Ché."

THE IMAGE BURNS

The way that after focusing
So long on fire
The image burns within
Or after staring so long
At a Sufi dervish
The mind begins to spin

So when our stare locks
Eyes and legs and breaths
Lunging in play
Yours is my shadow
On a sunlit day

Your earth and sky open
My mind replays
Your river through me
Heaving sweat waves
Your lips, your eyes
The image stays

INTO THE PROMISING

A Puerto Rican dad in a Phils cap
drinking a Bud with his shirt off,
sparkles like a wet brown tree
up to his knees in stream water,
a floating bucket tied to a belt loop
of his cut-offs. A chubby crane,
his beak fist plunges until his nose
touches the mirror, stares at himself
while his fingers pinch a pink
jewel from the clear underworld.
He tosses the crab into the pail
and looks at his kids splashing
like ducks upriver. His wife
readies a grill fire in the meadow.
I wave and he lifts the bucket,
tilts it into the sun so I can see
the same hundred squirming lunches
my father and I netted in creeks
stocked with muscled crawdads.
Far downstream, sunburned wasps
from the same Chestnut Hill estates
that loom over this fishing hollow
vacation at a shoreline crab stand
wielding mallets over newspaper
covered picnic tables — frenzied
sea gulls hammering their catch.
Their entire families turned to birds
with fish-filled gullets, both dads
will still break down and stop
for onion rings at the same fast food
drive-through my dad and I used to
visit on the way home. Then,
late at night with the kids in bed,
they'll stare, as mine did,
into the promising light
of their open refrigerators,
hungry for more time, more love:
that savory meat so thin and hard to get at,
as if wrapped with directions to a game,
protected by the prehistoric shell of ritual.

TO LIVE IN LOVE

Out beyond ideas of wrongdoing and rightdoing
there is a field. I'll meet you there.
~RUMI

All the other times that I was in Love, I was only visiting. I've passed through it many times and stayed in the hotels and visited the memorials and the amusement parks it's famous for and even found a few hidden places along the river that runs through it where I felt at home, but I've never stayed for long. I've never really been a resident of Love nor felt like I belonged there.

I've always secretly wanted a house in Love but could never afford one, or I was in a rush to get back to Hates, back to Jealousy, back to Good'nough, or to that old hammock bivouacked in the boughs of an old oak by the lemonade stand just outside of Settleforlessboro. Now that I see how things work in Love, I think I'd like to move in down here, buy some land, build a home, grow some vegetables and flowers. I think I'd like it in Love. I used to fear even stopping in Love. I thought I would be forced by the overpopulation and crime rate in Love to become coarse and defensive, set in my ways, or lose passion altogether. Most people who say they're in Love don't really live in Love anyway, but in some of the outlying suburbs: Possessiona, Adultery, Security Hills, East Custody, Xenophobia.

I want a plot and a loft right in the heated nexus of Love. I want to be one of those people you come visit in Love when you're growing up and you can't believe such a beautiful place exists but it does and it lets you know it does. A place to come home to. I want someone like you to live there in Love with me. Sure we'll go on vacations to the country of Passionata. Or we may have jobs in the Longing and Missing Islands. We'll still have relatives in Infermia, Boredomton, Mallville. But at least our kids'll be able to say they were born in Love and that they grew up there and that they know right where it is and feel at home in Love.